THE SECRET IS OUT

William Stanek is the artist behind the scenes at World Galleries, and the fiction author Robert Stanek.

BW Fall Arrives at Multnomah Falls in Canvas Print with Floating Frame

Find his art at 360 Studios

360studios.pictorem.com

williamrstanek.com

Note About the Front Matter

The front matter serves as an essential foundation for the series, ensuring that all readers—whether new to the books or returning after some time—can fully grasp the material. It introduces key concepts like the 8 Pillars of Intelligence and the Holistic Intelligence Model, both developed by William Stanek, providing critical context and continuity across the series. This consistent framework enables readers to engage deeply with the content, regardless of where they begin in the series.

For readers already familiar with these concepts, the option to skip directly to the main content is always available, allowing them to dive right into the heart of the book. This structure ensures accessibility for all, while respecting the time of experienced readers.

The Holistic Intelligence Model: The 8 Pillars of Personal and Professional Excellence

The 8 Pillars of Intelligence form the foundation of the Holistic Intelligence Model developed by William Stanek, a transformative framework designed to empower individuals in every dimension of life. This model transcends traditional notions of intelligence by encompassing eight distinct yet interconnected pillars: Emotional Resilience, Creativity Intelligence, Practical Intelligence, Cultural Intelligence, Intrapersonal Intelligence, Interpersonal Intelligence, Ethical Intelligence, and Analytical Intelligence. Each pillar represents a crucial dimension of human capability, addressing intellectual, emotional, ethical, and social competencies essential for thriving in today's dynamic and interconnected world.

At its core, the Holistic Intelligence Model emphasizes the synergy between these eight pillars, recognizing that true excellence arises from the harmonious development of diverse intelligences. By fostering resilience, creativity, practical problem-solving, cultural adaptability, self-awareness, interpersonal skills, ethical grounding, and analytical prowess, individuals are empowered to navigate complex challenges, build meaningful relationships, and achieve sustained success. This comprehensive approach ensures that personal growth is balanced across multiple facets of intelligence, promoting not only professional achievements but also overall well-being and fulfillment.

The model serves as a foundational guide for individuals seeking to enhance their capabilities in a structured and systematic manner. It provides actionable strategies and development pathways for each pillar, enabling continuous improvement and integration of these intelligences into daily life. Whether in leadership roles, creative endeavors, or personal relationships, the Holistic Intelligence Model equips individuals with the tools necessary to excel holistically, fostering a resilient, innovative, and ethically grounded mindset that drives meaningful impact and lasting success.

Pillar 1: Emotional Resilience (ER)

Emotional Resilience (ER) is the foundational pillar of the Holistic Intelligence Model, embodying the capacity to withstand and recover from emotional challenges and setbacks. It equips individuals with the strength to navigate adversity, maintain composure under pressure, and sustain a positive outlook despite difficulties. ER is not merely about bouncing back; it is about growing stronger and more adaptable through life's inevitable trials, thereby fostering long-term psychological well-being and stability.

The significance of Emotional Resilience extends across personal and professional domains. In the workplace, ER enhances performance by enabling individuals to manage stress effectively, stay focused on long-term goals, and lead teams with confidence during crises. Personally, it strengthens relationships by promoting empathy, effective communication, and the ability to support oneself and others through tough times. By cultivating ER, individuals build a robust emotional foundation that supports perseverance, adaptability, and proactive problem-solving, essential traits for sustained success and fulfillment.

Developing Emotional Resilience involves intentional practices such as mindfulness, self-compassion, and building strong social support networks. Strategies include embracing a growth mindset, enhancing coping skills through physical activity and stress management techniques, and fostering self-awareness through reflective practices. Practical applications of ER range from handling workplace stress and leading teams with composure to managing personal challenges and maintaining healthy relationships. By integrating ER with other intelligences, individuals can achieve a balanced and resilient approach to both personal growth and professional excellence.

Pillar 2: Creativity Intelligence (CrQ)

Creativity Intelligence (CrQ) is the pillar that fuels innovation, enabling individuals to generate unique ideas, solve problems innovatively, and adapt to changing environments with a creative mindset. CrQ encompasses a range of cognitive and emotional skills that facilitate the creation and implementation of novel concepts, processes, and products. It is essential for personal fulfillment and organizational success, fostering a culture of continuous improvement and adaptability.

The significance of Creativity Intelligence lies in its ability to drive progress and competitive advantage. In professional settings, CrQ leads to the development of new products, services, and processes that can differentiate an organization in the market. It enhances problem-solving by allowing individuals to approach challenges from unconventional angles, leading to more effective and sustainable solutions. Personally, CrQ contributes to a sense of achievement and satisfaction by enabling individuals to express their creativity and pursue innovative interests.

Enhancing Creativity Intelligence involves cultivating an explorative mindset, fostering adaptive thinking, and strengthening problem-solving proficiency. Strategies include engaging in creative activities, embracing playfulness, practicing divergent thinking, and seeking inspiration from diverse sources. Practical applications of CrQ range from leading innovation projects and strategic planning in the workplace to pursuing creative hobbies and personal goals in everyday life. By integrating CrQ with other intelligences, individuals can harness their creative potential to achieve both personal growth and professional excellence.

Pillar 3: Practical Intelligence (PQ)

Practical Intelligence (PQ), often referred to as "street smarts," is the ability to apply knowledge effectively in real-world situations. It bridges the gap between theoretical understanding and practical application, enabling individuals to navigate everyday complexities with confidence and efficiency. PQ encompasses skills such as effective decision-making, resource management, and adaptability, which are crucial for achieving tangible outcomes in both personal and professional contexts.

The significance of Practical Intelligence is evident in its impact on efficiency and effectiveness. In the workplace, PQ enhances project management, streamlines business processes, and supports strategic planning by ensuring that ideas are implemented successfully. It empowers individuals to solve problems pragmatically, optimize resources, and adapt to changing circumstances, thereby increasing productivity and reducing operational costs. Personally, PQ facilitates effective time management, financial planning, and home organization, contributing to a balanced and organized lifestyle.

Developing Practical Intelligence involves enhancing adaptability and flexibility, strengthening problem-solving and decision-making skills, and improving resource management and optimization. Strategies include engaging in scenario planning, utilizing decision-making frameworks, and practicing continuous improvement techniques. Practical applications of PQ range from managing business operations and executing strategic plans in the workplace to organizing daily tasks and achieving personal financial goals. By integrating PQ with other intelligences, individuals can ensure that their practical skills support their overall growth and success.

Pillar 4: Cultural Intelligence (CQ)

Cultural Intelligence (CQ) is the capability to relate and work effectively across diverse cultural settings. In an increasingly globalized world, CQ is essential for navigating multicultural environments, fostering inclusive workplaces, and building strong, respectful relationships with individuals from different cultural backgrounds. It involves understanding cultural norms, values, and communication styles, and adapting one's behavior to fit various cultural contexts.

The significance of Cultural Intelligence extends to both personal enrichment and professional success. In the workplace, CQ facilitates effective teamwork and collaboration in multicultural teams, enhances cross-cultural communication, and supports market expansion into new regions by understanding local consumer behaviors and business practices. Personally, CQ enriches interactions by promoting mutual respect, reducing misunderstandings, and fostering meaningful relationships with people from diverse backgrounds. It also contributes to personal growth by broadening perspectives and enhancing global awareness.

Enhancing Cultural Intelligence involves increasing cultural awareness, improving adaptability and flexibility, and developing empathy and social competence. Strategies include cultural education, immersion experiences, active listening, and empathy exercises. Practical applications of CQ range from leading multicultural teams and expanding businesses into international markets to building intercultural friendships and participating in diverse community activities. By integrating CQ with other intelligences, individuals can navigate cultural complexities with ease, fostering a harmonious and inclusive environment in all areas of life.

Pillar 5: Intrapersonal Intelligence (IntraQ)

Intrapersonal Intelligence (IntraQ), also known as Reflective Intelligence, is the capacity to understand oneself deeply. It encompasses self-awareness, self-regulation, and the ability to reflect on one's thoughts, emotions, and motivations. IntraQ is fundamental for personal growth, effective decision-making, and aligning actions with personal values and goals, providing a strong foundation for overall well-being and fulfillment.

The significance of Intrapersonal Intelligence lies in its role in fostering self-understanding and personal development. In the workplace, IntraQ enhances leadership by enabling leaders to understand their strengths and weaknesses, manage their emotions, and make decisions that are aligned with their values. It supports career development by helping individuals set clear goals and pursue them with intentionality and self-discipline. Personally, IntraQ contributes to emotional well-being by promoting self-compassion, resilience, and the ability to navigate personal challenges with clarity and purpose.

Developing Intrapersonal Intelligence involves cultivating self-awareness, enhancing emotional regulation, and fostering personal growth and self-reflection. Strategies include journaling, mindfulness meditation, and engaging in reflective practices that promote introspection and self-assessment. Practical applications of IntraQ range from setting and achieving personal goals and managing stress effectively to maintaining authentic relationships and pursuing continuous self-improvement. By integrating IntraQ with other intelligences, individuals can achieve a balanced and insightful approach to personal and professional excellence, ensuring that their actions are purposeful and aligned with their core values.

Pillar 6: Interpersonal Intelligence (InterQ)

Interpersonal Intelligence (InterQ), also known as Social Intelligence, is the ability to understand, communicate, and interact effectively with others. It involves recognizing and interpreting the emotions, motivations, and intentions of others, facilitating meaningful relationships and effective collaboration. InterQ is essential for leadership, teamwork, conflict resolution, and building a supportive social network, making it a critical component of the Holistic Intelligence Model.

The significance of Interpersonal Intelligence is evident in its impact on both personal relationships and professional environments. In the workplace, InterQ enhances team dynamics, fosters collaboration, and supports effective leadership by enabling individuals to inspire and motivate others. It facilitates client relations, conflict management, and networking, contributing to a positive and productive work culture. Personally, InterQ strengthens friendships, family bonds, and community connections by promoting empathy, effective communication, and mutual understanding, leading to more fulfilling and harmonious relationships.

Enhancing Interpersonal Intelligence involves developing empathy and social awareness, improving communication skills, and strengthening conflict management and negotiation abilities. Strategies include active listening, empathy exercises, and engaging in collaborative and team-building activities. Practical applications of InterQ range from leading diverse teams and building strong client relationships in the workplace to maintaining healthy friendships and family relationships in personal life. By integrating InterQ with other intelligences, individuals can foster a supportive and engaging social environment, enhancing both their personal well-being and professional success.

Pillar 7: Ethical Intelligence (EthQ)

Ethical Intelligence (EthQ) serves as the moral compass within the Holistic Intelligence Model, guiding individuals in making principled choices and maintaining integrity in all aspects of life. It involves understanding and adhering to ethical standards, promoting fairness, and demonstrating accountability and responsibility. EthQ is essential for building trust, fostering a positive reputation, and leading with integrity, ensuring that actions are aligned with moral values and societal expectations.

The significance of Ethical Intelligence is profound in both personal and professional contexts. In the workplace, EthQ enhances leadership by promoting ethical decision-making, integrity, and accountability, which are crucial for building trust and credibility within teams and organizations. It supports the development and enforcement of ethical policies, contributing to a culture of responsibility and fairness. Personally, EthQ ensures that individuals uphold their values in their interactions and decisions, fostering honest and trustworthy relationships and contributing positively to their communities.

Developing Ethical Intelligence involves clarifying personal values, enhancing ethical decision-making skills, and fostering integrity and accountability. Strategies include values clarification exercises, utilizing ethical decision-making frameworks, and engaging in continuous ethical education and reflection. Practical applications of EthQ range from leading with integrity and developing ethical policies in the workplace to maintaining honesty and fairness in personal relationships and community engagements. By integrating EthQ with other intelligences, individuals can ensure that their actions are not only effective and innovative but also morally sound and socially responsible, leading to sustained trust and respect.

Pillar 8: Analytical Intelligence (AQ)

Analytical Intelligence (AQ) is the ability to analyze complex problems, think critically, and make informed decisions based on evidence and logical reasoning. It involves breaking down information into manageable parts, identifying patterns, and synthesizing data to derive meaningful conclusions. AQ is essential for effective problem-solving, strategic planning, and informed decision-making in both personal and professional contexts, providing the cognitive tools necessary to navigate and excel in a data-driven world.

The significance of Analytical Intelligence lies in its role in enhancing decision-making and strategic thinking. In the workplace, AQ supports strategic planning by enabling individuals to analyze market trends, assess risks, and develop data-driven strategies that align with organizational goals. It enhances problem-solving capabilities by facilitating the identification of root causes and the development of effective solutions. Personally, AQ contributes to financial management, health tracking, and educational pursuits by enabling individuals to interpret data accurately and make informed decisions that promote well-being and success.

Developing Analytical Intelligence involves enhancing critical thinking, improving problem-solving skills, and strengthening data analysis and interpretation abilities. Strategies include engaging in critical thinking exercises, utilizing data analysis tools and software, and practicing reflective journaling on problem-solving experiences. Practical applications of AQ range from strategic business expansion and process optimization in the workplace to personal financial planning and health management in everyday life. By integrating AQ with other intelligences, individuals can ensure that their analytical capabilities support comprehensive and balanced growth, enabling them to make informed, ethical, and effective decisions across all areas of life.

Conclusion

The Holistic Intelligence Model offers a comprehensive and integrated approach to personal and professional development by encompassing eight pivotal pillars: Emotional Resilience, Creativity Intelligence, Practical Intelligence, Cultural Intelligence, Intrapersonal Intelligence, Interpersonal

Intelligence, Ethical Intelligence, and Analytical Intelligence. Each pillar addresses distinct aspects of human capability, ensuring that individuals develop a balanced and multifaceted intelligence that supports resilience, innovation, ethical integrity, and effective communication. This holistic framework recognizes the interconnectedness of diverse intelligences, emphasizing that true excellence is achieved through the harmonious growth of all these dimensions.

By cultivating each of these eight pillars, individuals are empowered to navigate complex challenges, build meaningful relationships, and achieve sustained success and fulfillment. The model provides actionable strategies and development pathways, enabling continuous improvement and the integration of these intelligences into daily life. Whether in leadership roles, creative endeavors, or personal relationships, the Holistic Intelligence Model equips individuals with the tools necessary to excel holistically, fostering a resilient, innovative, and ethically grounded mindset.

Ultimately, the Holistic Intelligence Model serves as a guiding framework for individuals seeking to enhance their capabilities in a structured and systematic manner. By embracing and developing each pillar, individuals can achieve comprehensive intelligence and excellence, leading to meaningful impact and lasting success in all areas of life. Embrace this model as a transformative journey towards balanced growth, personal fulfillment, and professional achievement.

Letter from the Author

In the realm of leadership and intelligence, there exists a tapestry woven from the threads of experience, wisdom, and an unyielding commitment to excellence. This tapestry has been crafted over the course of three decades, each thread representing a moment of triumph, a lesson learned, or a challenge met head-on. It is a privilege to share these threads with you, dear reader, as we embark on a journey through the corridors of leadership, guided by the principles of the Holistic Intelligence Model.

In these pages, you will discover not only a roadmap to effective leadership but also a comprehensive framework that integrates Emotional Resilience, Creativity Intelligence,

Practical Intelligence, Cultural Intelligence, Intrapersonal Intelligence, Interpersonal Intelligence, Ethical Intelligence, and Analytical Intelligence. These eight pillars form the foundation of a multifaceted intelligence that transcends traditional measures, enabling leaders to navigate complex landscapes with adaptability, innovation, and integrity.

As we delve into the nuances of each pillar, you will gain insights into how these interconnected intelligences work in synergy to foster resilient and dynamic leadership. Whether it's harnessing Emotional Resilience to maintain composure under pressure, leveraging Creativity Intelligence to drive innovation, or applying Ethical Intelligence to uphold integrity, each pillar offers practical strategies and profound wisdom. Together, they unlock doors to innovation, adaptability, and enduring success, providing a holistic approach to leadership that is both practical and inspiring.

This book is not merely a collection of ideas but a distillation of a lifetime's worth of experiences, framed within the Holistic Intelligence Model. It is an offering to leaders, both seasoned and aspiring, who seek to cultivate a balanced and integrated intelligence that supports sustained excellence and fulfillment. It is my sincerest hope that you will find within these pages not only practical guidance but also inspiration to lead with purpose, passion, and resilience, embodying the essence of holistic intelligence in every endeavor.

In the crucible of leadership, one discovers not only the power to guide and influence but also the profound responsibility that comes with it. Over three decades at the intersection of technology, business, and leadership, I have gleaned insights that have shaped my approach to leadership intelligence. From navigating pivotal historical moments to addressing complex technological challenges, these experiences have reinforced the importance of a balanced and integrated intelligence framework.

Throughout my career as a technology consultant and leader, I have learned that the heart of many seemingly insurmountable problems lies not in technological failings but in the nuanced dynamics of leadership and intelligence. This revelation became the cornerstone of my approach, emphasizing that effective leadership is a multifaceted endeavor encompassing Emotional Resilience, Practical Intelligence, Ethical Intelligence, and the other pillars of holistic intelligence. By embracing this integrated framework, leaders can inspire, influence, and adeptly guide teams through even the most formidable challenges.

In this book, and indeed throughout this series, I invite you to embark on a journey of discovery, exploring the intricacies of leading with purpose, adaptability, and a commitment to growth. Together, we will harness the power of holistic intelligence to achieve greater effectiveness, impact, and resilience. May these pages serve as a compass on your own leadership journey, guiding you towards balanced growth and meaningful success.

With warm regards,

William R. Stanek.

Our Foundational Proposition: Navigating the Complex Tapestry of Success

In a world saturated with discussions on various intelligences, our perspective transcends the oversimplified dichotomy of emotional intelligence (EQ) versus intellectual intelligence (IQ). While acknowledging the undeniable importance of emotional intelligence, our exploration delves deeper, recognizing the intricate interplay of the eight pillars of the Holistic Intelligence Model—Emotional Resilience, Creativity Intelligence, Practical Intelligence, Cultural Intelligence, Intrapersonal Intelligence, Interpersonal Intelligence, Ethical Intelligence, and Analytical Intelligence—within the tapestry of effective living and success.

Consider the story of Temple Grandin, a renowned scientist and advocate for individuals with autism. Her unique perspective and creative problem-solving have revolutionized the livestock industry. Grandin's journey reflects the intersection of Practical Intelligence, Emotional Resilience, and Creativity Intelligence, showcasing the versatile dimensions crucial for life, success, and leadership. Similarly, visionaries like Elon Musk demonstrate the indispensable role of Practical Intelligence and Analytical Intelligence in achieving monumental feats. Musk's relentless commitment to innovation highlights how these intelligences synergize to propel progress, rather than overshadow one another.

Meet Frances Arnold, a groundbreaking chemist and engineer awarded the Nobel Prize in Chemistry. Her journey of innovation showcases not only Analytical Intelligence but also Emotional Resilience in a field where women were historically underrepresented. Arnold's creative problem-solving and tenacity redefine the boundaries of intelligence in life, success, and leadership, embodying the harmonious blend of multiple intelligences that drive profound achievements. Steve Jobs, with his unparalleled Analytical Acumen and Creativity Intelligence, demonstrated that visionary success goes beyond emotional intelligence. His ability to distill complex ideas into user-friendly solutions revolutionized industries, emphasizing the symbiotic relationship between Analytical Intelligence and Creativity Intelligence.

Dikembe Mutombo, a former NBA star turned philanthropist, exemplifies the power of Interpersonal Intelligence and Emotional Resilience in life, success, and leadership. Through his humanitarian efforts, Mutombo exhibits an unwavering commitment to uplifting communities, showcasing how Emotional Intelligence and Ethical Intelligence can drive impactful social change. Bill Gates, a luminary in strategic foresight and business acumen, exemplifies the pivotal role of Analytical Intelligence and Practical Intelligence in life, success, and leadership. His capacity to envision the future and strategically navigate challenges underscores the indispensable nature of Holistic Intelligence.

Consider the story of Kip Thorne, a theoretical physicist who played a pivotal role in the discovery of gravitational waves. His ability to navigate ambiguity in the pursuit of groundbreaking discoveries exemplifies the fusion of Analytical Intelligence and Creativity Intelligence, setting an extraordinary example for those working in dynamic environments. Ai Weiwei, a Chinese artist and activist, exemplifies leadership through Creative Intelligence and Ethical Intelligence. His courage in challenging societal norms and fostering change highlights the transformative power of creativity combined with ethical discernment.

Intelligence, we argue, is a multidimensional tapestry that extends beyond the realms of EQ and IQ. The narrative expands to encompass luminaries like Michelle Obama, whose Emotional Resilience has been instrumental in navigating the complexities of public life; Winston Churchill's tenacity reflecting Emotional Resilience and Analytical Intelligence; Indra Nooyi's resourcefulness showcasing Practical Intelligence; Oprah Winfrey's self-belief embodying Intrapersonal Intelligence; Warren Buffett's analytical prowess highlighting Analytical Intelligence; Tim Cook's mindset shifting illustrating Cognitive and Emotional Flexibility; and Malala Yousafzai's challenge reframing, which integrates Ethical Intelligence and Emotional Resilience. These figures collectively weave a narrative that defies simplistic categorizations, embodying the holistic integration of multiple intelligences for impactful existence.

Our proposition revolves around the dynamic interplay of these diverse intelligences, each contributing uniquely to the tapestry of success. It is a paradigm that acknowledges the multifaceted strengths of individuals who excel not by adhering to a rigid framework but by skillfully navigating the intricate dance of the eight pillars of Holistic Intelligence. These exemplars, each embodying specific resilient characteristics, illustrate the power of a multidimensional approach to intelligence. The constellation of essential intelligences for triumphant existence encompasses ethical discernment, cultural acumen, creative ingenuity, relational adeptness, and more, forming a symphony that forges the crucible of true excellence.

This holistic fusion, a testament to the boundless potential of human intellect, breathes life into visionary endeavors, shaping the course of personal and professional journeys, and inspiring generations to come. In our journey to reimagine leadership and success, we must transcend the limiting paradigm of EQ versus IQ. Instead, let us embrace the Holistic Intelligence Model—a comprehensive framework that recognizes and celebrates the manifold facets of intelligence. Through this lens, we equip ourselves to tackle the complexities of modern life with nuance, wisdom, and unwavering determination, fostering a balanced and integrated approach to achieving unparalleled success.

Acknowledgements

Embarking on this journey of exploring the Holistic Intelligence Model and its application to leadership has been a profound experience, one that has been shaped by the guidance and support of numerous individuals. First and foremost, I extend my deepest gratitude to the Chief Officers of Fortune 100, 500, and 1000 companies who entrusted me with their most complex challenges. Your unwavering faith in my ability to devise solutions in seemingly impossible situations has been both humbling and empowering, providing real-world contexts in which the pillars of Emotional Resilience, Practical Intelligence, and Ethical Intelligence have been tested and refined.

I am indebted to the countless leaders I've had the privilege to work alongside throughout my career. Each interaction, each challenge faced together, has contributed to the insights and principles shared in this book. Your dedication to excellence, your unwavering commitment to your teams, and your willingness to embrace innovation have been a constant source of inspiration, highlighting the critical roles of Interpersonal Intelligence and Cultural Intelligence in effective leadership.

To my colleagues and mentors, both past and present, thank you for your invaluable guidance and wisdom. Your collective expertise and diverse perspectives have enriched my understanding of the eight pillars of Holistic Intelligence. It is through our collaborations that many of the concepts explored in these pages have taken shape, particularly in areas such as Analytical Intelligence and Creativity Intelligence, which have been instrumental in developing robust strategies for leadership and personal growth.

I extend a special thanks to those who have provided feedback and insights during the development of this book. Your thoughtful contributions have been instrumental in refining the ideas and ensuring their accessibility to a wide audience. Your willingness to engage in discussions, challenge assumptions, and share your own experiences has been invaluable in shaping the Ethical and Practical aspects of the Holistic Intelligence Model.

This book is a testament to the collective wisdom of leaders, past and present, who have left an indelible mark on the world. It is a tribute to the countless individuals who have demonstrated that leadership is not defined by titles, but by actions, by the impact we have on those we serve. It is a celebration of the potential that lies within each of us to lead with purpose, compassion, and a commitment to positive change, guided by the comprehensive framework of Holistic Intelligence.

Finally, to my family, whose unwavering support has been a constant source of strength, thank you for standing by my side throughout this endeavor. Your belief in me and in the importance of this work has been a driving force. This book is as much a reflection of your encouragement as it is of my own journey through the eight pillars of Holistic Intelligence.

With deepest gratitude,

William R. Stanek

Building Resilience Foundations

Lay the cornerstone for leadership that thrives under pressure.

Elevating Skills, Mindsets, and Strengths for Transformational Leadership in Your Personal and Professional Life

Includes a 2-week Action Plan for Leaders

William Stanek's Leadership Intelligence Mastery Series

William R. Stanek
Author & Series Creator

William Stanek's Leadership Intelligence Mastery Series

Elevating Skills, Mindsets, and Strengths for Transformational Leadership in Your Personal and Professional Life

Building Resilience Foundations

Lay the cornerstone for leadership that thrives under pressure.

Published by Stanek & Associates
in conjunction with
Big Blue Sky Press for Business
www.williamrstanek.com.

Copyright © 2025 William R. Stanek. Seattle, Washington. All rights reserved. Photographs of the author are © HC Stanek. Fine-art photographs and illustrations are © William R. Stanek and were created by the author.

No part of this book may be reproduced, stored in a retrieval system or transmitted in any form or by any means, electronic, mechanical, photocopying, recording, scanning or otherwise, except as permitted by Sections 107 or 108 of the 1976 United States Copyright Act, without the prior written permission of the publisher Requests to the publisher for permission should be sent to the address listed previously.

Stanek & Associates is a trademark of Stanek & Associates and/or its affiliates. All other marks are the property of their respective owners. No association with any real company, organization, person or other named element is intended or should be inferred through use of company names, web site addresses or screens.

This book expresses the views and opinions of the author. The information contained in this book is provided without any express, statutory or implied warranties.

LIMIT OF LIABILITY/DISCLAIMER OF WARRANTY: THE PUBLISHER AND THE AUTHOR MAKE NO REPRESENTATIONS OR WARRANTIES WITH RESPECT TO THE ACCURACY OR COMPLETENESS OF THE CONTENTS OF THIS WORK AND SPECIFICALLY DISCLAIM ALL WARRANTIES, INCLUDING WITHOUT LIMITATION WARRANTIES OF FITNESS FOR A PARTICULAR PURPOSE. NO WARRANTY MAY BE CREATED OR EXTENDD BY SALES OR PROMOTIONAL MATERIALS. THE ADVICE AND DISCUSSION IN THIS BOOK MAY NOT BE SUITABLE FOR EVERY SITUATION. THIS WORK IS SOLD WITH THE UNDERSTANDING THTAT THE PUBLISHER IS NOT ENGAGED IN RENDERING PROFESSIONAL SERVICES AND THAT SHOULD PROFESSIONAL ASSISTANCE BE REQUIRED THE SERVICES OF A COMPETENT PROFESSIONAL SHOULD BE SOUGHT. NEITHER THE PUBLISHERS, AUTHORS, RESELLERS NOR DISTRIBUTORS SHALL BE HELD LIABLE FOR ANY DAMAGES CAUSED OR ALLEGED TO BE CAUSE EITHER DIRECTLY OR INDIRECTLY HEREFROM. THE REFERENCE OF AN ORGANIZATION OR WEBSITE AS A SOURCE OF FURTHER INFORMATION DOES NOT MEAN THAT THE PUBLISHER OR

THE AUTHOR ENDORSES THE INFORMATION THE ORGANIZATION OR WEBSITE MAY PROVIDE OR THE RECOMMENDATIONS IT MAY MAKE. FURTHER, READERS SHOULD BE AWARE THAT WEBSITES LISTED IN THIS BOOK MAY NOT BE AVAILABLE OR MAY HAVE CHANGED SINCE THIS WORK WAS WRITTEN.

Stanek & Associates publishes in a variety of formats, including print, electronic and by print-on-demand. Some materials included with standard print editions may not be included in electronic or print-on-demand editions or vice versa.

Country of First Publication: United States of America.

Cover Design: Creative Designs Ltd.
Editorial Development: Andover Publishing Solutions
Content & Technical Review: L & L Technical Content Services

You can provide feedback related to this book by emailing the author at williamstanek @ aol.com. Please use the name of the book as the subject line.

1st Edition. Version: 1.0.1.0b

> **Note** I may periodically update this text and the edition and version number shown previously will let you know which version you are working with. If there's a specific feature you'd like me to write about in an update, message me on Facebook (http://facebook.com/williamstanekauthor). Please keep in mind readership of this book determines how much time I can dedicate to it.

Special Notice for Groups and Teams Are you part of a group or team seeking comprehensive Empowered Leadership© and Inspirational Journeys© training? We offer tailored programs for groups of 12 or more, designed to equip you with the tools and strategies needed to thrive in today's dynamic landscape. Discover the power of collective growth and resilience! For inquiries and customized solutions, please reach out to Jeannie Kim jeannie.kim @ reagentpress.com.

Bulk Orders Available Looking to equip your team or organization with the transformative power of the "Leadership Intelligence Mastery" books? We offer special pricing and customized packages for bulk orders. For more information and to place your order, please contact Jeannie Kim jeannie.kim @ reagentpress.com.

Epigraph

In *The Resilient Leader*, we quoted Nelson Mandela:

> "The greatest glory in living lies not in never falling, but in rising every time we fall." - Nelson Mandela

You might be surprised to learn that Confucius expressed this same idea—more than 2,400 years earlier.

> "Our greatest glory is not in never falling, but in rising every time we fall." – Confucius

This striking parallel highlights the enduring nature of this wisdom. The belief that true strength lies not in avoiding failure but in rising after a fall transcends time, culture, and context. It's a universal truth that has been recognized and articulated by thinkers, philosophers, and leaders throughout history.

This shared understanding speaks to a profound truth about the human experience: resilience and perseverance are timeless virtues. They form the foundation for growth, leadership, and transformation, no matter the era or setting.

This timeless wisdom lies at the core of our exploration of emotional resilience and leadership excellence, serving as a reminder that the principles we study today are deeply rooted in the shared human journey.

Table of Contents

Note About the Front Matter 2
The Holistic Intelligence Model: The 8 Pillars of Personal and Professional Excellence 3
Letter from the Author 15
Our Foundational Proposition: Navigating the Complex Tapestry of Success 18
Acknowledgements 22
Epigraph 30
Table of Contents 31
Part 1. Let's Get Started! 39
    The 8 Pillars of Intelligence As a Framework for Transformative Leadership 40
    Opening Reflection 44
Charting Your Leadership Course 47
Building Resilience Foundations 51
Thriving Through Resilience: A 2-Week Action Plan 53
Instructions for the Action Plan 63
Resilience Foundations: Exploring Key Concepts 69
    Introduction to Emotional Resilience in Leadership 70
        The Limitations of Problem-Solving Alone 70
        Emotional Resilience: A Comprehensive Approach ... 71
        Navigating Ambiguity and Uncertainty 73
        Balancing Empathy with Personal Boundaries 73

- Emotional Regulation in High-Pressure Situations 74
- Fostering a Growth Mindset 74
- Integrating Emotional Resilience with Problem-Solving . 75
- Case Study: Emotional Resilience in Action 75
- Emotional Resilience in Leadership 77
  - Enhancing Decision-Making 81
  - Building Trust and Inspiring Confidence 82
  - Promoting Adaptability and Embracing Change 83
  - Effective Communication and Emotional Intelligence 84
  - Cultivating a Positive Organizational Culture 85
  - Handling Criticism and Maintaining Integrity 86
  - Navigating Crises with Composure 86
  - Promoting Holistic Well-Being Through Emotional Resilience 87
  - Leading by Example 88
- How Emotional Resilience Complements Other Leadership Skills 89
  - Enhancing Effective Communication 106
  - Strengthening Empathy and Building Trust 107
  - Navigating Team Dynamics and Conflict Resolution 107
  - Enhancing Decision-Making Abilities 108
  - Inspiring and Motivating Teams 108
  - Facilitating Adaptability and Embracing Change 109
  - Empowering Through Effective Delegation 109
  - Upholding Integrity and Ethical Leadership 110
  - Enhancing Time Management and Prioritization 110
  - Fostering a Culture of Learning and Innovation 111

Enhancing Customer Relationships 111
Promoting Inclusive Leadership 112
Strengthening Leadership Presence 112
Enabling Responsible Risk-Taking 113
Empowering Others 113
Promoting Accountability 113
Balancing Empathy with Boundaries 114

The Impact of Emotional Resilience on Leadership Effectiveness 116
Boosting Team Motivation and Productivity 117
Cultivating a Resilient Organizational Culture 118
Promoting Innovation and Creativity 119
Strengthening Relationships with Stakeholders 120
Enhancing Personal Well-being and Sustainable Leadership 120
Fostering Team Cohesion and Collaboration 121
Adapting to Change and Uncertainty 121

Improved Decision-Making under Pressure 122
Enhancing Decision-Making Under Pressure 124
Maintaining Composure 125
Strategic Thinking 126
Balancing Emotions and Logic 127
Case Study: Narendra Modi 127
Instilling Confidence Through Resilient Leadership 128

Enhancing Team Motivation and Productivity 130
The Leader as an Emotional Anchor 130
The Contagious Nature of Resilience 131

Leadership Mastery | 33

    Recognizing and Valuing Individual Contributions 131

    Creating a Psychologically Safe Environment 132

    The Negative Impact of Lacking Emotional Resilience ... 133

    Case Study: Emotional Resilience in Action 133

  Creating a Positive Work Culture and Atmosphere: 135

    Fostering a Growth Mindset 137

    Prioritizing Well-Being and Self-Care 137

    Cultivating Inclusivity and Diversity 138

    Leading by Example 140

    Building Psychological Safety 140

    Avoiding Negative Cultural Impacts 141

  Strategies for Leaders to Enhance Emotional Resilience ... 142

  Strategies to Cultivate Emotional Resilience in Organizations 143

Case Study 1: The Resilient Leader in Action 145

  Analyzing Key Situations Showcasing Emotional Resilience 146

  Extracting Actionable Insights and Strategies 147

Guided Self-Assessment: A Personal Reflection 150

  Evaluating Current Level of Emotional Resilience 152

  Identifying Areas for Growth and Development 155

  Setting Personalized Goals for the Journey Ahead 156

Cultivating Foundational Resilience Traits 159

  1. Self-Awareness 159

  2. Adaptability 161

  3. Proactive Problem-Solving 162

  4. Inner Strength 163

Integrating Foundational Traits: Strategies for Development **165**
    1. Embrace Change as an Opportunity 165
    2. Practice Mindful Awareness 165
    3. Seek Constructive Solutions 166
    4. Draw on Past Resilience 166
    5. Cultivate a Growth Mindset 167
    6. Cultivate a Supportive Network 167
    Example in Practice: 168

Building a Resilient Mindset **171**
    1. Shifting from Reactive to Proactive 171
    2. Embracing Challenges as Opportunities for Growth 173
    3. Cultivating a Forward-Thinking Perspective 174

Strategies to Cultivate a Resilient Mindset **177**
    1. Practice Mindfulness and Reflection 177
    2. Set Clear Goals and Objectives 178
    3. Anticipate Challenges and Contingencies 179
    4. Foster a Learning Culture 180
    5. Embody Adaptability and Flexibility 182
    6. Celebrate Small Wins 183

Resilience as a Leadership Competency **186**
    1. Recognizing Emotional Resilience as a Critical Leadership Skill 186
    2. Impact on Decision-Making 187
    3. Influence on Team Dynamics 189
    4. Contribution to Organizational Success 190

Developing Emotional Resilience as a Leadership Competency 192

Fostering Emotional Resilience in Your Team 195

The Importance of Cultivating a Culture of Resilience 195

Creating a Supportive Environment 200

The Impact of Fostering Emotional Resilience 202

Case Study 2: The Resilient Leader in Action 204

Analyzing Key Instances Demonstrating Resilience in Leadership 206

Extracting Insights and Strategies from the Case Study 208

Lessons in Resilience from Björn Johansson's Leadership Style 211

Practical Takeaways for Leaders Seeking Resilience in Leadership 214

Leadership Case Reviews: Mastering Situations in Building Resilience 218

Tools and Techniques for Enhancing Resilience in Leadership 223

1. Stress Management Practices 223

2. Cultivating a Growth Mindset 224

3. Time Management and Prioritization 225

4. Building a Support Network 226

5. Emotional Regulation Techniques 227

6. Adaptive Decision-Making 228

7. Effective Communication Skills 229

8. Resilience-Building Workshops and Training 229

9. Conflict Resolution Skills 230

10. Crisis Response Planning 231

11. Continuous Learning and Skill Development................... 232
12. Self-Care Practices.. 233
13. Reflective Practice... 233
14. Delegation and Empowerment 234
15. Scenario Planning and Contingency Preparation.......... 235
16. Feedback-Seeking Behavior 236
17. Cognitive Flexibility... 237
18. Practicing Self-Compassion 238
19. Empathy and Active Listening... 238
20. Celebrating Successes.. 239

Thoughtful Exploration: Building Resilience Foundations 242

About the Author: William R. Stanek............................. 245

Biography... 246
Connect with William R. Stanek.. 247

Part 1. Let's Get Started!

Leadership Intelligence Mastery is a groundbreaking series that delves into the evolving landscape of leadership in the 21st century. It challenges the prevailing notion that Emotional Intelligence (EQ) and Intellectual Intelligence (IQ) alone suffice in the complex world of modern leadership. Instead, it introduces the Holistic Intelligence Model, a comprehensive framework that integrates eight essential pillars—Emotional Resilience (ER), Creativity Intelligence (CrQ), Practical Intelligence (PQ), Cultural Intelligence (CQ), Intrapersonal Intelligence (IntraQ), Interpersonal Intelligence (InterQ), Ethical Intelligence (EthQ), and Analytical Intelligence (AQ)—to redefine effective leadership.

In a rapidly changing global economy, leaders are tasked with navigating a myriad of challenges that demand more than traditional intelligence metrics. Leadership Intelligence Mastery recognizes that the divide between EQ and IQ is insufficient. By incorporating the eight pillars of the Holistic Intelligence Model, this series provides a robust framework that goes beyond conventional boundaries of intelligence. At its core, the books spotlight Emotional Resilience (ER) as the linchpin of effective leadership, equipping leaders to bounce back from setbacks, manage stress, and maintain a positive outlook even in the face of adversity.

Moreover, the series carefully dissects the distinctions between Emotional Resilience and EQ, emphasizing that ER transcends and encompasses emotional intelligence. It delves into the cognitive processes associated with understanding and managing emotions in high-pressure scenarios. By introducing the eight pillars of intelligence, including Creativity Intelligence (CrQ) for driving innovation, Cultural Intelligence (CQ) for leading in a globalized world, and Ethical Intelligence (EthQ) for principled leadership, Leadership Intelligence Mastery offers a holistic approach that empowers leaders to thrive in every dimension of their roles.

The 8 Pillars of Intelligence As a Framework for Transformative Leadership

As a Framework for Transformative Leadership, the 8 Pillars of Intelligence represent a revolutionary approach, combining a diverse array of skills and perspectives that empower leaders to excel in today's dynamic environments. These pillars—Emotional Resilience (ER), Creativity Intelligence (CrQ), Practical Intelligence (PQ), Cultural Intelligence (CQ), Intrapersonal Intelligence (IntraQ), Interpersonal Intelligence (InterQ), Ethical Intelligence (EthQ), and Analytical Intelligence (AQ)—transcend traditional notions of intelligence, shaping leaders who are resilient, innovative, and impactful. Together, they form a foundation for a transformative leadership journey that is as practical as it is profound.

1. Emotional Resilience (ER): The Keystone of Leadership

Emotional Resilience is the core pillar that empowers leaders to remain composed under pressure, recover quickly from setbacks, and sustain a positive and focused outlook. It transcends traditional emotional intelligence, embodying a level of emotional fortitude that helps leaders face challenges with grace and inspire confidence in others.

2. Creativity Intelligence (CrQ): Driving Vision and Innovation

Creativity Intelligence equips leaders with the ability to think beyond boundaries, generate novel ideas, and adapt to change. This pillar is vital for problem-solving, fostering innovation, and guiding teams toward visionary solutions. Leaders with high CrQ turn challenges into opportunities for growth and transformation.

3. Practical Intelligence (PQ): Bridging Knowledge and Action

Practical Intelligence—sometimes referred to as "street smarts"—helps leaders effectively apply their knowledge to real-world situations. It emphasizes adaptability, resourcefulness, and sound decision-making in dynamic environments, ensuring that leadership strategies are actionable and results-oriented.

4. Cultural Intelligence (CQ): Leading in a Globalized World

Cultural Intelligence allows leaders to thrive in diverse and interconnected environments. By fostering a deep understanding of cultural norms, values, and practices, this pillar enables leaders to build authentic connections, foster inclusivity, and navigate cross-cultural dynamics with sensitivity and skill.

5. Intrapersonal Intelligence: Leading from Within

Intrapersonal Intelligence focuses on self-awareness and self-regulation, enabling leaders to understand their own emotions, motivations, and values. This pillar empowers leaders to align their actions with their purpose, making decisions rooted in authenticity and inspiring trust among their teams.

6. Interpersonal Intelligence: The Art of Influence and Connection

Interpersonal Intelligence helps leaders build meaningful relationships, foster collaboration, and navigate social dynamics effectively. With strong interpersonal skills, leaders can communicate clearly, resolve conflicts constructively, and create an environment of trust and mutual respect, driving team cohesion and shared purpose.

7. Ethical Intelligence (EthQ): Leadership with Integrity

Ethical Intelligence serves as the moral foundation for principled leadership. By upholding values such as honesty, accountability, and fairness, leaders with strong ethical intelligence make decisions that inspire trust, maintain credibility, and prioritize the greater good. This pillar is essential for building an ethical and sustainable leadership legacy.

8. Analytical Intelligence (AQ): Solving Complexity with Clarity

Analytical Intelligence equips leaders with critical thinking and problem-solving skills needed to make sound, evidence-based decisions. By discerning patterns, evaluating risks, and analyzing data, leaders with strong analytical intelligence navigate complexity with precision and deliver effective, strategic outcomes.

A Symphony of Interconnected Intelligences

Embracing the Holistic Intelligence Model means embarking on a transformative journey where each pillar contributes uniquely to your leadership narrative. Whether you are stepping into a new leadership role, facing unprecedented challenges, or seeking to enhance your personal growth, the eight pillars provide a comprehensive roadmap to guide your path. Integrate Emotional Resilience (ER) to maintain composure and inspire your team during turbulent times, leverage Creativity Intelligence (CrQ) to drive innovation and strategic vision, and apply Practical Intelligence (PQ) to translate ideas into actionable plans. Enhance your leadership effectiveness by cultivating Cultural Intelligence (CQ) to navigate globalized environments, Intrapersonal Intelligence (IntraQ) for self-awareness and authentic decision-making, Interpersonal Intelligence (InterQ) to build strong, collaborative relationships, Ethical Intelligence (EthQ) to uphold integrity and trust, and Analytical Intelligence (AQ) to solve complex problems with clarity and precision.

Together, these pillars form a symphony of intelligences that empower you to lead with resilience, creativity, practicality, cultural sensitivity, self-awareness, interpersonal adeptness, ethical integrity, and analytical prowess. As you integrate these facets into your leadership practice, you will not only excel in your roles but also inspire those around you to achieve their fullest potential, creating a legacy of impactful and sustainable leadership.

Opening Reflection

Before you continue, take a moment to center yourself with the photograph that follows.

As you gaze upon this Hawaiian horizon, where the sun meets the sea, envision your leadership journey stretching out before you. Like the rhythmic crash of waves against the rocky shoreline, your path may be marked by challenges, yet it is also adorned with moments of beauty and triumph. Just as the sun dips below the horizon, signaling the close of one day and the promise of another, your journey in leadership is a series of endings and beginnings. Embrace them all, for they are the threads that weave the tapestry of your growth and resilience.

The interplay of light and shadow in this Hawaiian sky mirrors the dynamic nature of leadership. Each experience, each decision, shapes your narrative, much like the shifting colors of the sky influence the mood of the moment. With each step, you etch your unique story into the sands of time, drawing upon the eight pillars of the Holistic Intelligence Model—from Emotional Resilience (ER) that provides strength during tumultuous times to Creativity Intelligence (CrQ) that sparks innovative solutions. Let the spirit of the islands infuse your path with vitality and inspiration, empowering you to lead with purpose, passion, and resilience.

In this moment, on this shore, you stand at the threshold of a transformative journey. Let the timeless beauty of this photograph serve as a beacon, guiding you back to the essence of your leadership journey. Just as the boardwalk stretches ahead, disappearing into the horizon, your leadership odyssey is filled with boundless opportunities and unforeseen turns. Embrace each step with curiosity and purpose, knowing that every challenge met and every triumph celebrated is a testament to your strength and resilience. Embrace the path, for it is uniquely yours to shape, guided by the comprehensive framework of the Holistic Intelligence Model.

And if ever the winds of uncertainty threaten to steer you off course, return to this photograph. Let the timeless beauty of this moment serve as a beacon, guiding you back to the essence of your leadership journey. Remember, every challenge met, every triumph celebrated, is a testament to your strength and resilience. Embrace the path, for it is uniquely yours to shape.

When faced with crossroads, remember this mountain road. It symbolizes the choices, the uncharted territories, and the possibilities that await. As you stand at the precipice of decisions, know that each step, even the uncertain ones, contributes to your leadership odyssey. Embrace the journey, for every turn leads to growth, to wisdom, to your unique legacy. Keep forging ahead, for the road not taken is the one that defines your extraordinary story.

Charting Your Leadership Course

My journey through the intricacies of leadership has unfolded amidst some of the most pivotal moments in modern history. From the tense era of the Cold War to the turbulent times of the Iraq War, I found myself navigating through significant conflicts that tested our nation's resilience. What distinguishes me is my exceptional ability not only to adapt but to thrive in these high-pressure environments. Time and again, I was thrust into senior leadership positions, defying my relatively junior rank. This speaks volumes about my knack for evaluating critical situations and skillfully guiding those around me—often individuals significantly senior to me—toward resounding success, grounded in the eight pillars of the Holistic Intelligence Model.

My experiences, shaped in the crucible of the military and other arenas, have granted me profound insights: genuine leadership surpasses mere titles or years of service. It revolves around the ability to inspire and influence, to steer a team through even the most daunting challenges. In my role as a technology consultant, I often assumed the mantle of the "fixer" – the one summoned when situations seemed dire and hope was fading. Surprisingly, I discovered that more often than not, the root cause of many seemingly insurmountable problems was not a technological failure but rather a breakdown in leadership and intelligence dynamics. This realization reinforced the importance of Emotional Resilience

(ER), Interpersonal Intelligence (InterQ), and Analytical Intelligence (AQ) in effective leadership.

Recognizing this recurring pattern, my consulting focus naturally evolved toward uncovering people-centric solutions. It became evident that the success of any endeavor, particularly in the fast-paced and constantly evolving landscape of technology, hinges on the human element. This revelation forms the foundation of the principles expounded in our book, emphasizing that effective leadership is a multifaceted endeavor encompassing Emotional Resilience (ER), Practical Intelligence (PQ), Ethical Intelligence (EthQ), and the other pillars of holistic intelligence. By delving into the human dynamics that underpin every facet of professional life, our book provides a comprehensive guide for individuals looking to excel in their roles and lead with authenticity, empathy, and strategic acumen. Through a series of exercises, case studies, reflective practices, and more, readers will gain invaluable insights into honing their own intelligences, fostering a deeper understanding of themselves and those they lead.

Ultimately, this book is a testament to the idea that true leadership is a holistic endeavor, requiring a keen awareness of oneself, an astute understanding of others, and an unwavering commitment to ethical and principled decision-making. It's a call to action for leaders at every level and in every industry to embrace the complexities of human dynamics and harness them as a force for positive change and lasting success. Together, let us embark on this journey of reimagining leadership intelligence, shaping a future where leadership transcends convention and inspires profound transformation.

As you step into this transformative phase, remember that every milestone, every challenge, and every triumph is a thread woven into the tapestry of your leadership journey. Embrace each moment with curiosity and purpose, for it is through this journey that you will discover the true depth of your leadership potential. Let the Holistic Intelligence Model guide you, ensuring that your leadership is resilient, innovative, ethical, and profoundly impactful.

Let your gaze linger on the boardwalk that stretches ahead, disappearing into the horizon. Much like this path, your leadership journey unfurls before you, an odyssey filled with boundless opportunities and unforeseen turns. The distant pagoda-like structure beckons, a symbol of your destination, a testament to your aspirations.

Embrace the ebb and flow, for just as the tides shape the estuary, experiences shape leadership. The interplay of shadows and light in the sky above mirrors the dynamic nature of challenges and triumphs you'll encounter. Each step is a stitch in the fabric of your leadership narrative, weaving together resilience, wisdom, and growth.

With every footfall, you write your own story of leadership. As you traverse this boardwalk, know that you carry with you the potential to create profound impact. The journey itself is your canvas, waiting for the brush strokes of your unique vision. Embrace it with an open heart and a steadfast spirit, for the path you walk is yours to shape and yours to own.

Building Resilience Foundations

Thriving Through Resilience: A 2-Week Action Plan

Embarking on the journey to enhance your emotional resilience as a leader requires intentional effort and structured guidance. This 2-week action plan is designed to help both aspiring leaders and seasoned professionals grasp, apply, and integrate the principles outlined in our book, "Emotional Resilience in Leadership." The plan offers a balanced mix of reading, reflection, practical exercises, and application of tools and techniques, all while providing the flexibility to tailor it to your specific needs and aspirations.

Week 1: Building the Foundation of Emotional Resilience

Day 1: Introduction and Orientation

- **Objective:** Familiarize yourself with the action plan and set intentions for the upcoming two weeks.
- **Time Allocation:** 1-2 hours
- **Actions:**
- Review the Table of Contents: Understand the structure and key themes of the book.
- Read The Holistic Intelligence Model, Letter From the Author and Our Foundational Proposition to understand the unique approach of the book.
- Read Introduction to Emotional Resilience in Leadership
- Set Personal Goals: Define what you aim to achieve through this action plan.
- Start a Gratitude Journal: Dedicate 15 minutes to note things you are grateful for to cultivate a positive mindset.

Day 2: Emotional Resilience in Leadership
- **Objective:** Grasp the fundamental concepts of emotional resilience and its role in effective leadership.
- **Time Allocation:** 2-3 hours
- **Actions:**
- Read Emotional Resilience in Leadership
- Summarize Key Points: Reflect on how emotional resilience impacts leadership effectiveness.
- Journal Your Insights: Spend 15 minutes writing about your initial thoughts and how these concepts relate to your leadership style.

Day 3: How Emotional Resilience Complements Other Leadership Skills
- **Objective:** Understand how emotional resilience enhances and integrates with other essential leadership skills.
- **Time Allocation:** 2-3 hours
- **Actions:**
- Read How Emotional Resilience Complements Other Leadership Skills
- Reflect on Integration: Consider how emotional resilience interacts with each of these leadership skills.
- Journal Your Reflections: Document examples from your experience where emotional resilience has complemented these skills.

Day 4: The Impact of Emotional Resilience on Leadership Effectiveness
- **Objective:** Explore the various ways emotional resilience enhances leadership effectiveness.
- **Time Allocation:** 2-3 hours

- **Actions:**
- Read The Impact of Emotional Resilience on Leadership Effectiveness
- Analyze the Case Study: Read and reflect on the example of Narendra Modi.
- Apply Insights: Think about how these impacts manifest in your own leadership context.
- Journal Your Thoughts: Record key takeaways and potential applications.

Day 5: Enhancing Team Motivation and Productivity

- **Objective:** Learn strategies to boost team motivation and productivity through emotional resilience.
- **Time Allocation:** 2-3 hours
- **Actions:**
- Read Enhancing Team Motivation and Productivity
- Identify Strategies: Note down specific strategies that can enhance your team's motivation and productivity.
- Plan Implementation: Choose at least two strategies to implement within your team.
- Journal Your Plans: Document how you will apply these strategies and expected outcomes.

Day 6: Creating a Positive Work Culture and Atmosphere

- **Objective:** Understand how to cultivate a positive and resilient work culture.
- **Time Allocation**: 2-3 hours
- **Actions:**
- Read Creating a Positive Work Culture and Atmosphere
- Analyze Current Culture: Assess the current work culture within your team or organization.

- Identify Improvements: Highlight areas where a more positive and resilient culture can be fostered.
- Plan Actions: Develop a plan to implement cultural improvements.
- Journal Your Reflections: Record insights and action steps.

Day 6: Exploring Case Study 1: The Resilient Leader in Action

- **Objective:** Learn from real-life examples of resilient leadership.
- **Time Allocation:** 1.5 – 2.5 hours
- **Action:**
- Read and analyze Case Study 1: The Resilient Leader in Action.
- Extract key strategies and lessons learned.
- Reflect on how these strategies can be integrated into your leadership approach.
- Journal your reflections and action points.

Day 7: Guided Self-Assessment and Weekly Reflection

- **Objective:** Evaluate your progress and consolidate learnings from Week 1.
- **Time Allocation:** 1.5 – 2 hours
- **Actions:**
- Complete Guided Self-Assessment: A Personal Reflection
- Review Journal Entries: Reflect on your notes and insights from the week.
- Summarize Key Learnings: Highlight the most impactful concepts and strategies.
- Adjust Personal Goals: Refine your development goals based on your reflections.

- Celebrate Achievements: Acknowledge your progress and set intentions for Week 2.

Week 2: Applying Tools, Techniques, and Fostering Team Resilience

Day 8: Cultivating Foundational Resilience Traits
- **Objective:** Develop essential traits that form the foundation of emotional resilience.
- **Time Allocation:** 2-3 hours
- **Actions:**
- Read Cultivating Foundational Resilience Traits
- Reflect on Each Trait: Consider how each trait manifests in your leadership and identify areas for improvement.
- Engage in Exercises: Perform exercises related to self-awareness and adaptability.
- Journal Your Reflections: Document your understanding and personal development plans for each trait.

Day 9: Integrating Foundational Traits: Strategies for Development
- **Objective:** Apply strategies to develop and strengthen foundational resilience traits.
- **Time Allocation:** 2-3 hours
- **Actions:**
- Read Integrating Foundational Traits: Strategies for Development
- Implement Strategies: Choose at least two strategies to focus on this week.
- Apply in Daily Life: Begin integrating these strategies into your routine.

- Journal Your Experiences: Track how these strategies impact your resilience.

Day 10: Building a Resilient Mindset
- **Objective:** Develop a resilient mindset to proactively handle challenges.
- **Time Allocation:** 2-3 hours
- **Actions:**
- Read Building a Resilient Mindset
- Reflect on Mindset Shifts: Assess how shifting from reactive to proactive can enhance your leadership.
- Set Mindset Goals: Define specific goals to cultivate a resilient mindset.
- Journal Your Reflections: Document your mindset shifts and plans for integration.

Day 11: Strategies to Cultivate a Resilient Mindset
- **Objective:** Apply strategies to strengthen your resilient mindset.
- **Time Allocation:** 2-3 hours
- **Actions:**
- Read Strategies to Cultivate a Resilient Mindset
- Implement Strategies: Choose at least two strategies to focus on this week.
- Apply in Leadership Role: Begin integrating these strategies into your daily leadership practices.
- Journal Your Experiences: Track your progress and insights.

Day 12: Resilience as a Leadership Competency
- **Objective:** Recognize and develop emotional resilience as a critical leadership competency.

- **Time Allocation:** 2-3 hours
- **Actions:**
- Read Resilience as a Leadership Competency
- Analyze Leadership Competencies: Identify how emotional resilience integrates with other leadership skills.
- Develop a Competency Plan: Create a plan to enhance emotional resilience as a core competency.
- Journal Your Reflections: Document your competency development plan and expected outcomes.

Day 13: Fostering Emotional Resilience in Your Team

- **Objective:** Implement strategies to cultivate emotional resilience within your team.
- **Time Allocation:** 2-3 hours
- **Actions:**
- Read Fostering Emotional Resilience in Your Team
- Develop a Team Resilience Plan: Outline specific actions to foster resilience within your team.
- Implement Strategies:

    - Lead by Example: Demonstrate emotional resilience in your actions.

    - Promote Open Communication: Encourage team members to discuss challenges and seek support.

    - Provide Resources and Training: Offer workshops or training programs focused on resilience.

- Journal Your Actions: Record the strategies you implemented and the team's response.

Day 13: Exploring Case Study 2: The Resilient Leader in Action

- **Objective:** Learn from real-life examples of resilient leadership.
- **Time Allocation:** 1.5 – 2.5 hours
- **Action:**
- Read and analyze Case Study 2: The Resilient Leader in Action.
- Extract key strategies and lessons learned.
- Reflect on how these strategies can be integrated into your leadership approach.
- Journal your reflections and action points.

Day 14: Tools and Techniques for Enhancing Resilience in Leadership

- **Objective:** Master various tools and techniques to further enhance your emotional resilience as a leader.
- **Time Allocation:** 2-3 hours
- **Actions:**
- Read Tools and Techniques for Enhancing Resilience in Leadership
- Select Key Tools: Identify which tools and techniques resonate most with your needs.
- Create an Action Plan: Develop a plan to incorporate these tools into your leadership practice.
- Implement and Reflect: Begin using these tools and document their effectiveness.
- Journal Your Insights: Record how these tools impact your resilience and leadership.

Tools and Resources

To support your journey through this action plan, consider leveraging the following tools and resources:

- **Journaling Apps:** Tools like Day One, Evernote, or Microsoft OneNote to document your reflections, insights, and progress.
- **Mindfulness Apps:** Applications such as Headspace, Calm, or Insight Timer for guided meditation and mindfulness exercises.
- **Goal-Setting Worksheets:** Templates to define and track your personal development goals, available on platforms like Canva or Google Docs.
- **Books by William Stanek:** Dive deeper into leadership and personal development by exploring the Leadership Intelligence Mastery Library by William Stanek. These books provide invaluable insights and practical strategies to enhance your growth and understanding.
- **Resilience Workshops:** Participate in or organize workshops focused on building emotional resilience and adaptive thinking.

Final Thoughts

Building emotional resilience is an ongoing journey that extends beyond these two weeks. Use this action plan as a foundation to develop and strengthen your resilience continuously. By committing to these practices, you not only enhance your own leadership capabilities but also inspire and empower your team to develop their own resilience. This collective strength contributes to a more adaptable, innovative, and high-performing organization capable of thriving in the face of adversity.

Next Steps:
- Review and Adjust the Action Plan: Tailor the activities to better fit your personal and professional schedule.
- Engage Your Team: Share this action plan with your team members to foster a collective commitment to resilience.
- Track Your Progress: Use your gratitude journal and personal development plan to monitor your growth and make necessary adjustments.
- Seek Continuous Improvement: Regularly revisit the strategies and tools discussed in the book to further enhance your emotional resilience.

By following this 2-week action plan, you lay a strong foundation for integrating emotional resilience into your leadership role, setting the stage for enduring success and a thriving organizational culture.

Instructions for the Action Plan

The action plan offers a structured approach to integrate the strategies discussed in this book into your leadership style, whether you're starting your leadership journey or looking to enhance your existing leadership skills.

While the action plan is initially structured as a two-week schedule, it's important to note that both the schedule and all other aspects of the plan can be fully customized to align with your individual needs and preferences:

- **Personalization**   Tailor the suggested activities to align with your current level of leadership experience, preferences, and specific leadership context.

- **Allocate Flexible Time**   Recognize that the suggested schedule and time allocations are flexible. Adjust them to accommodate your availability and preferences. Focus on quality engagement rather than rigid adherence to schedules and time frames.

- **Reflect and Internalize**   After completing each session or activity, take time to reflect on the insights gained. Internalize how they can be applied to your unique leadership challenges and opportunities.

As an added component, contemplate including the following optional activities as part of the action plan:

- **Discussion Forums**   Engage with fellow leaders in discussions related to the content. Share experiences, insights, and challenges for mutual learning. This platform caters to leaders at various stages of their careers.

- **Weekly Q&A Sessions**   Attend live Q&A sessions to seek clarifications, share progress, and gain additional guidance from peers and experts. These sessions are beneficial for both aspiring leaders and experienced professionals looking to exchange insights.

- **Resource Library**   Explore the supplementary materials provided to deepen your understanding and application of resilience concepts. This resource is valuable regardless of your level of leadership experience.

Here are some overarching tips to assist you on your journey:

- **Consistency is Key**   Engage consistently with the material and activities to embed resilience practices into your leadership style, regardless of your current leadership level.

- **Balance Learning and Application**   Strike a balance between learning from the book and actively applying the concepts in your leadership role. This approach is beneficial for leaders at all stages.

- **Document Progress**   Keep a journal to record your reflections, insights, and challenges. Track your growth in resilience over time. This practice is valuable for leaders at any point in their journey.

- **Seek Feedback**   Encourage open communication with your team or peers. Seek feedback on your leadership style and adjust your approach based on their input. This applies to leaders at any stage of their careers.

- **Stay Open-Minded**   Embrace new ideas and perspectives. Be open to adapting your leadership style based on the insights gained. This attitude is crucial for leaders at all levels.

- **Celebrate Milestones**   Acknowledge and celebrate your achievements, no matter how small. Recognize your growth in resilience. This practice is relevant for leaders at any stage of their careers.

By following the structured action plan, you will not only gain a deeper understanding but also develop practical skills. The journey towards transformative leadership is ongoing, and each step you take contributes to your continued growth and development, regardless of your level of experience.

For aspiring leaders when the action plans suggest applying concepts to your leadership role, keep the following in mind:

- **Understand the Concept**   Begin by thoroughly understanding the concept or principle outlined in the action plan. Take time to grasp its significance and how it contributes to effective leadership.

- **Reflect on Relevance**   Consider how this concept applies to your current leadership aspirations and goals. Reflect on specific situations or scenarios where you can implement this principle.

- **Identify Opportunities**   Even if you haven't held formal leadership positions yet, there are likely opportunities within your academic, professional, or personal life where you can exhibit leadership qualities. Look for chances to take initiative, influence others positively, or demonstrate resilience.

- **Experiment and Practice**   Apply the concept in these identified opportunities. Experiment with different approaches and observe the outcomes. Pay attention to what works well and what may require adjustments.

- **Seek Feedback**   Don't hesitate to ask for feedback from mentors, supervisors, or peers who have experience in leadership roles. Their insights can provide valuable guidance on how you can further develop and apply these leadership skills.

- **Reflect on Learnings**   After applying the concept, take time to reflect on the experience. Consider what went well, what challenges you faced, and what you learned from the process.

- **Document Achievements**   Keep a record of instances where you successfully applied the concept. This documentation serves as tangible evidence of your developing leadership abilities and can be valuable when discussing your leadership potential in future endeavors.

- **Continuously Learn and Adapt**   Aspire to be a lifelong learner. Stay open to new ideas and seek opportunities for growth. Adapt your approach based on the insights gained from applying leadership concepts.

Leadership is not solely defined by titles or formal positions. As an aspiring leader, you have the capacity to demonstrate leadership qualities in various capacities. Embrace these opportunities to cultivate and showcase your leadership potential. Each step you take now lays the foundation for your future leadership journey.

Lastly, whether you're an aspiring leader or an experienced one, keep the following points in mind:

- **Consistency and Patience** Developing leadership skills is a journey that requires consistency and patience. It's important to acknowledge that growth takes time, and each step forward, no matter how small, is a valuable progression.

- **Adaptability** Leadership is a dynamic field, and the ability to adapt to changing circumstances and environments is crucial. Remain open to new ideas, feedback, and emerging trends in leadership.

- **Leverage Networks** Building a network of mentors, peers, and industry contacts can provide valuable insights and opportunities for growth. Don't hesitate to seek advice or engage in discussions with others who have experience in leadership.

- **Embrace Failure** Failure is a natural part of the learning process. It's important to view setbacks as opportunities for growth and learning. Embrace challenges, learn from mistakes, and use them as stepping stones toward future success.

- **Self-Care and Well-Being** Effective leadership starts with taking care of oneself. Prioritize physical, emotional, and mental well-being to ensure you have the energy and resilience needed to lead effectively.

- **Setting Personal Goals**   Consider setting specific, measurable goals related to your leadership development. These goals can provide a clear direction for your journey and serve as milestones to track your progress.

- **Seek Additional Resources**   Beyond the book, there are numerous resources available to support leadership development. This may include workshops, courses, seminars, and industry-specific publications. Stay curious and explore these opportunities.

- **Reflection and Continuous Improvement**   Regularly take time to reflect on your leadership journey. Consider what has been effective, areas for improvement, and the direction you want to take in your leadership development.

- **Celebrate Achievements**   Acknowledge and celebrate your achievements, no matter how small. Recognizing your progress can boost confidence and motivation, reinforcing your commitment to leadership growth.

- **Stay Inspired**   Find sources of inspiration that resonate with you. Whether it's books, TED talks, podcasts, or biographies of influential leaders, seek out content that fuels your passion for leadership.

Leadership is a multifaceted skill that evolves over time. Embrace the process, stay committed to your growth, and remain open to new experiences and knowledge. The journey toward becoming an effective leader is not only professionally fulfilling but also personally enriching.

Resilience Foundations: Exploring Key Concepts

In the ever-evolving landscape of leadership, the ability to weather storms and emerge stronger on the other side is not just a desirable trait – it's a necessity. Here, we lay the cornerstone for the journey ahead, delving into the fundamental aspects of building emotional resilience. It is here that we explore the essence of what makes a leader not only withstand adversity but thrive amidst it.

Emotional resilience, often described as the capacity to bounce back from challenges, is more than a skill; it's a mindset. It encompasses a rich tapestry of attributes, from adaptability and problem-solving to inner strength and cognitive adaptability. Understanding these components forms the bedrock of leadership in the 21st century.

Through tangible strategies, thought-provoking insights, and real-world case studies, we equip leaders with the tools to enhance their emotional resilience. By examining the experiences of a resilient leader, we gain valuable insights into the practical application of these strategies in the professional sphere.

We encourage introspection and personal development. Leaders are invited to embark on a journey of self-assessment, identifying areas of strength and opportunities for growth. By setting tailored goals for their resilience journey, leaders can begin to cultivate the attributes that will fortify them in the face of adversity.

Join us on this foundational exploration of emotional resilience – a journey that promises not only to bolster leadership effectiveness but also to foster personal growth and well-being. Together, we will uncover the keys to thriving in the complexities of the modern leadership landscape.

Introduction to Emotional Resilience in Leadership

In the dynamic realm of leadership, navigating challenges effectively requires more than just adept problem-solving skills. While problem-solving is an essential cognitive ability focused on identifying solutions to specific issues, emotional resilience emerges as a multifaceted response that integrates emotional, cognitive, and behavioral elements. It acknowledges that challenges often evoke complex emotional reactions and that leaders must engage with these emotions constructively to lead successfully.

The Limitations of Problem-Solving Alone

Problem-solving is inherently task-oriented, aiming to address immediate obstacles through logical reasoning and analytical thinking. It involves:

- **Defining the Problem:** Identifying the specific issue at hand.

- **Generating Solutions:** Brainstorming possible ways to tackle the problem.
- **Evaluating Options:** Assessing the feasibility and potential outcomes of each solution.
- **Implementing Actions:** Executing the chosen solution to resolve the issue.

While this approach is valuable, it often overlooks the human element—how emotions, stress, and interpersonal dynamics influence both the leader and their team. Solely relying on problem-solving can lead to solutions that are technically sound but fail to address underlying emotional or cultural factors that may affect long-term success.

Emotional Resilience: A Comprehensive Approach

In contrast, emotional resilience equips leaders to not only overcome immediate challenges but also to thrive amid ongoing adversity. It involves cultivating inner strength and stability, fostering a deep-rooted belief in one's capacity to weather difficulties, and maintaining composure regardless of external pressures. Emotional resilience emphasizes:

1. Emotional Awareness and Regulation

- **Self-Awareness:** Recognizing and understanding one's own emotions, triggers, and responses.
- **Empathy:** Being attuned to the emotions of others, which enhances communication and relationship-building.
- **Emotional Regulation:** Managing emotional reactions to prevent them from negatively impacting decision-making or team dynamics.

Example: A leader who receives negative feedback might initially feel defensive. Through emotional resilience, they recognize this reaction, regulate their response, and use the feedback constructively.

2. Adaptability and Cognitive Flexibility

- **Open-Mindedness:** Being willing to consider new ideas and perspectives.
- **Learning Agility:** Quickly absorbing new information and applying it effectively.
- **Adjusting Strategies:** Modifying plans in response to changing circumstances.

Example: During a sudden market shift, an adaptable leader pivots the business strategy to meet new customer demands rather than clinging to outdated models.

3. Long-Term Perspective and Growth Mindset

- **Seeing the Big Picture:** Understanding how current challenges fit into overall goals.
- **Embracing Challenges:** Viewing obstacles as opportunities for learning and development.
- **Persistence:** Maintaining effort and enthusiasm despite setbacks.

Example: A project fails to meet its objectives. Instead of viewing it as a total loss, the resilient leader analyzes what can be learned to improve future initiatives.

Navigating Ambiguity and Uncertainty

Leaders often face situations filled with ambiguity, where information is incomplete and outcomes are uncertain. Emotional resilience enables leaders to:

- **Maintain Composure Under Pressure:** Staying calm allows for clearer thinking and better decision-making.
- **Embrace Uncertainty:** Accepting that not all variables can be controlled and finding ways to move forward despite unknowns.
- **Informed Decision-Making:** Balancing intuition and analysis when making decisions without all the facts.

Example: During a crisis, an emotionally resilient leader reassures their team, communicates transparently about uncertainties, and focuses on controllable actions.

Balancing Empathy with Personal Boundaries

An emotionally resilient leader understands the importance of supporting others while also safeguarding their own well-being:

- **Empathy and Compassion:** Fostering a supportive environment by understanding team members' perspectives and feelings.
- **Setting Healthy Boundaries:** Recognizing when to step back to prevent burnout, ensuring personal emotional health is maintained.
- **Encouraging Self-Care:** Promoting practices that support mental and emotional well-being within the team.

Example: A leader notices a team member is overworked. They offer support and resources while also delegating tasks to prevent personal overload.

Emotional Regulation in High-Pressure Situations

High-pressure situations can trigger intense emotional responses. Emotional resilience involves:

- **Self-Regulation Techniques:** Utilizing mindfulness, deep breathing, or reflective practices to manage stress.
- **Rational Composure:** Keeping emotions in check to maintain objectivity and clear judgment.
- **Modeling Calmness:** Demonstrating steady leadership that reassures and stabilizes the team.

Example: In the face of a public relations crisis, the leader addresses the issue calmly, provides clear guidance, and sets a tone of confidence and control.

Fostering a Growth Mindset

Emotional resilience fosters a growth mindset by encouraging leaders to:

- **Embrace Challenges:** Viewing difficulties as opportunities to develop new skills and insights.
- **Learn from Failure:** Treating setbacks as valuable learning experiences.
- **Cultivate Optimism:** Maintaining a positive outlook focused on possibilities rather than limitations.

Example: After a failed product launch, the leader gathers insights, motivates the team to innovate further, and maintains confidence in future success.

Integrating Emotional Resilience with Problem-Solving

While problem-solving addresses the "what" and "how" of challenges, emotional resilience addresses the "why" and "who." Integrating both allows leaders to:

- **Approach Challenges Holistically:** Combining strategic thinking with emotional intelligence for more effective solutions.
- **Enhance Team Dynamics:** Understanding and managing emotional undercurrents that impact performance.
- **Achieve Sustainable Success:** Building a foundation for long-term achievement by fostering resilience in themselves and their teams.

Example: In implementing organizational change, the leader not only plans the logistical steps but also addresses team members' concerns and emotions, ensuring smoother adoption and engagement.

Case Study: Emotional Resilience in Action

Scenario: Laura, a senior manager at a tech firm, faces a significant project setback due to a vendor's failure to deliver critical components on time. The delay jeopardizes a major product launch.

Problem-Solving Approach:

Immediate Actions: Laura quickly searches for alternative vendors and adjusts project timelines.

Focus: Solely on finding a solution to meet the launch deadline.

Emotional Resilience Approach:

Emotional Acknowledgment: Recognizes her own frustration and disappointment, as well as her team's stress.

Team Support: Holds a meeting to address concerns, provide reassurance, and refocus the team's efforts.

Adaptability: Adjusts the project's scope where possible and communicates transparently with stakeholders.

Growth Mindset: Encourages the team to view the setback as an opportunity to improve processes and vendor management.

Outcome:

By integrating emotional resilience with problem-solving, Sarah not only addresses the immediate issue but also strengthens team cohesion, improves morale, and enhances future project management practices.

In conclusion, emotional resilience transcends mere problem-solving by encompassing a wider array of attributes essential for effective leadership in complex and high-pressure environments. It is not a replacement for problem-solving skills but a crucial complement that enriches a leader's capacity to navigate adversity. Developing emotional resilience alongside problem-solving equips leaders with a comprehensive toolkit for personal growth and professional excellence.

In the ever-evolving landscape of leadership, cultivating emotional resilience enables leaders to:

- **Lead with Empathy and Strength:** Balancing emotional understanding with decisive action.
- **Navigate Complexity with Confidence:** Handling uncertainty and ambiguity with poise.
- **Inspire and Empower Others:** Modeling resilience that encourages teams to adopt similar mindsets.

By embracing emotional resilience, leaders position themselves and their organizations not just to survive challenges but to transform them into catalysts for innovation and growth.

Emotional Resilience in Leadership

Leadership, by its very nature, often entails navigating a landscape fraught with complexity, ambiguity, and high-pressure scenarios. In this dynamic environment, the significance of emotional resilience cannot be overstated. It emerges as a linchpin for leaders, providing them with the capacity to maintain effectiveness, make well-informed decisions, and inspire unwavering confidence in their teams.

Within the context of leadership, where the stakes are often high, emotional resilience takes center stage. It serves as the cornerstone for leaders seeking to not only weather the storm but to do so with an air of composure and adaptability. These qualities, in turn, set a powerful example for the entire organizational ecosystem, demonstrating that even in the face of adversity, steadfastness and effectiveness can prevail.

The nexus between emotional resilience and effective leadership is perhaps most conspicuous in the realm of decision-making. Here, the presence or absence of emotional resilience can fundamentally alter the course of action taken by a leader. An emotionally resilient leader possesses the capacity for clear-headed assessments, ensuring that decisions are made judiciously, particularly in high-stakes situations where the margin for error is razor-thin.

Emotional resilience introduces a crucial equilibrium into the decision-making process. It prompts leaders to weigh not only the practical considerations but also the emotional undercurrents that may influence outcomes. This balanced perspective allows for decisions that are not only effective in achieving desired objectives but also attuned to the emotional well-being of team members.

In the crucible of leadership, trust is the bedrock upon which successful endeavors are built. Emotional resilience plays an instrumental role in engendering and upholding this trust. When leaders demonstrate unwavering composure and adaptability in the face of adversity, they send a powerful message to their teams – one that reassures them that their leader is not swayed by external pressures, but instead remains resolute in the pursuit of shared goals.

An emotionally resilient leader fosters an environment where team members feel safe and supported. This psychological safety net encourages open communication, constructive dissent, and a willingness to take calculated risks. As a result, the entire team operates in an atmosphere of trust, confident in their leader's ability to navigate any challenges that may arise.

In an era marked by rapid change and uncertainty, adaptability has emerged as a cornerstone of effective leadership. Emotional resilience equips leaders with the ability to not only weather change but to do so with grace and an eye towards opportunity. By showcasing adaptability, leaders serve as living embodiments of the organizational culture they seek to foster – one that embraces change as a catalyst for growth rather than a harbinger of instability.

Leaders who exhibit emotional resilience in the face of change set a powerful example for their teams. They demonstrate that in an ever-evolving landscape, agility and adaptability are not mere buzzwords, but rather essential qualities that empower individuals and organizations to thrive.

Communication lies at the heart of effective leadership. An emotionally resilient leader possesses the capacity to communicate with clarity, authenticity, and empathy – even in the most challenging of circumstances. This ability stems from a foundation of emotional stability, allowing leaders to convey their messages with unwavering confidence and a keen understanding of their team's needs and perspectives.

Emotional resilience enables leaders to navigate difficult conversations with finesse. Whether delivering constructive feedback or addressing sensitive issues, an emotionally resilient leader approaches such interactions with a focus on solutions and a commitment to maintaining the integrity of relationships.

A leader's influence extends far beyond the confines of the professional realm; it permeates the personal lives of team members. An emotionally resilient leader recognizes the significance of holistic well-being and takes proactive steps to promote it. By prioritizing mental, emotional, and physical health, leaders create an environment where team members feel valued, supported, and empowered to bring their best selves to their professional roles.

An emotionally resilient leader encourages a culture that destigmatizes mental health concerns and fosters an atmosphere of open dialogue. This, in turn, paves the way for team members to seek support and resources when needed, ultimately contributing to a healthier, more productive work environment.

In the complex arena of leadership, emotional resilience emerges as a cornerstone, underpinning effective decision-making, inspiring confidence and trust, setting an example of adaptability, facilitating effective communication, and promoting a culture of holistic well-being. It is not merely a desirable trait, but an essential quality that distinguishes leaders who thrive in the face of adversity. As we embark on this exploration of emotional resilience, we do so with the understanding that its significance in the realm of leadership is profound and far-reaching.

Enhancing Decision-Making

At the heart of leadership lies decision-making. In high-pressure situations, emotions such as fear, anxiety, or frustration can cloud judgment, leading to impulsive or overly cautious choices. Emotional resilience empowers leaders to manage these emotional responses, maintaining a clear and objective mindset. This capacity for self-regulation ensures that decisions are grounded in rational analysis rather than reactive impulses.

Emotional resilience introduces a crucial equilibrium into the decision-making process. It prompts leaders to weigh not only practical considerations but also the emotional undercurrents that may influence outcomes. This balanced perspective allows for decisions that effectively achieve objectives while also being attuned to the emotional well-being of team members.

Emotionally resilient leaders can manage stress and anxiety, preventing these emotions from clouding their judgment. They are able to assess situations objectively, weigh options carefully, and make informed decisions even under duress. This capacity is crucial in high-stakes scenarios where impulsive decisions can lead to adverse outcomes.

Example: Angela Merkel

- Angela Merkel, the former Chancellor of Germany, is renowned for her calm and steady leadership during numerous crises, including the European financial crisis, the migrant crisis, and the COVID-19 pandemic. Her ability to remain composed under pressure and make rational decisions earned her the nickname "The Crisis Manager." Merkel's emotional resilience allowed her to navigate complex political landscapes, balancing national interests with European unity. Her methodical approach to problem-solving and her capacity to withstand criticism exemplify how emotional resilience enhances leadership effectiveness.

Building Trust and Inspiring Confidence

Trust is the bedrock upon which successful leadership is built. Emotional resilience plays an instrumental role in cultivating and upholding this trust. When leaders demonstrate unwavering composure and adaptability in the face of adversity, they send a powerful message to their teams—that they are not swayed by external pressures but remain resolute in pursuing shared goals.

Emotionally resilient leaders foster environments where team members feel safe and supported. This psychological safety encourages:

- **Open Communication:** Team members feel comfortable sharing ideas and concerns.
- **Constructive Dissent:** Healthy debates lead to better solutions.
- **Calculated Risk-Taking:** Innovation thrives when failure is seen as a learning opportunity.

Leaders who exhibit emotional resilience foster trust within their teams and organizations. By maintaining composure and demonstrating consistency in their actions and decisions, they create a sense of stability. Team members are more likely to have confidence in leaders who can handle adversity without becoming overwhelmed.

Example: Winston Churchill

- During World War II, British Prime Minister Winston Churchill displayed remarkable emotional resilience. Faced with the threat of invasion and relentless bombings, Churchill remained steadfast, delivering speeches that inspired courage and determination among the British people. His unwavering resolve and ability to project confidence in the face of immense adversity were instrumental in maintaining national morale. Churchill's leadership illustrates how emotional resilience can inspire confidence and unite people during challenging times.

Promoting Adaptability and Embracing Change

The modern world is characterized by rapid changes and uncertainties. Emotional resilience equips leaders with the ability to not only weather change but to embrace it with grace and an eye toward opportunity. By showcasing adaptability, leaders serve as living embodiments of the organizational culture they seek to foster—one that views change as a catalyst for growth rather than a threat.

Leaders who exhibit emotional resilience in the face of change demonstrate that agility and adaptability are essential qualities that empower individuals and organizations to thrive. They encourage a culture where continuous learning and flexibility are valued, equipping their organizations to stay competitive and innovative.

Not only are emotionally resilient leaders better equipped to adapt to new circumstances and guide their organizations through transitions, they view challenges as opportunities for growth rather than insurmountable obstacles.

Example: Emmanuel Macron

- As President of France, Emmanuel Macron has faced various challenges, including economic reforms, social unrest, and the COVID-19 pandemic. Macron's ability to adapt his strategies in response to changing conditions demonstrates emotional resilience. He has navigated complex political environments, proposing reforms to modernize the French economy while addressing public concerns. His willingness to adjust policies and communicate transparently with citizens reflects an adaptable leadership style grounded in resilience.

Effective Communication and Emotional Intelligence

Effective communication lies at the heart of successful leadership. An emotionally resilient leader possesses the capacity to communicate with clarity, authenticity, and empathy—even in the most challenging circumstances. This ability stems from a foundation of emotional stability, allowing leaders to convey their messages with unwavering confidence and a keen understanding of their team's needs and perspectives.

Emotionally resilient leaders excel in:

- **Active Listening:** They genuinely seek to understand others' viewpoints.
- **Empathetic Responses:** They acknowledge emotions and validate concerns.
- **Transparent Communication:** They share information openly, building trust.

Emotional resilience enables leaders to navigate difficult conversations with finesse. Whether delivering constructive feedback or addressing sensitive issues, they approach such interactions with a focus on solutions and a commitment to maintaining the integrity of relationships.

Example: Ursula von der Leyen

- As President of the European Commission, Ursula von der Leyen has been at the forefront of the European Union's response to various challenges, including Brexit negotiations and the COVID-19 crisis. Her ability to communicate effectively with member states, balancing different perspectives while promoting unity, showcases her emotional resilience. Von der Leyen's empathetic approach and commitment to collaboration have been crucial in navigating complex political dynamics within the EU.

Cultivating a Positive Organizational Culture

Leaders with emotional resilience contribute to creating a supportive and resilient organizational culture. They model behaviors that encourage openness, collaboration, and mutual support. This environment enables teams to cope better with stress and change.

Example: Sanna Marin

- Sanna Marin, the former Prime Minister of Finland, became the world's youngest serving prime minister at the age of 34. Her leadership style emphasizes collaboration, transparency, and inclusivity. Marin has demonstrated emotional resilience in handling both domestic issues and international relations, promoting policies that focus on social welfare and sustainability. Her approach fosters a positive culture within her government, encouraging innovation and adaptability.

Handling Criticism and Maintaining Integrity

Leaders often face scrutiny and criticism. Emotional resilience enables them to handle negative feedback constructively without compromising their integrity or vision.

Example: Margrethe Vestager

- As the European Commissioner for Competition, Margrethe Vestager has taken on major multinational corporations over antitrust issues, including imposing significant fines on tech giants. Despite facing criticism and pressure from various stakeholders, Vestager has remained steadfast in enforcing competition laws. Her emotional resilience allows her to uphold her principles and carry out her duties effectively, maintaining integrity in the face of challenges.

Navigating Crises with Composure

During crises, emotionally resilient leaders can guide their organizations through uncertainty, providing direction and reassurance.

Example: Mette Frederiksen

- Mette Frederiksen, the Prime Minister of Denmark, has been recognized for her effective leadership during the COVID-19 pandemic. Her decisive actions and transparent communication helped Denmark respond swiftly to the crisis. Frederiksen's emotional resilience was evident in her ability to make tough decisions while maintaining public trust. By leading by example, she fostered a collective sense of responsibility among citizens.

Promoting Holistic Well-Being Through Emotional Resilience

A leader's influence extends beyond professional realms; it permeates the personal lives of team members. Emotionally resilient leaders recognize the significance of holistic well-being and take proactive steps to promote it. By prioritizing mental, emotional, and physical health, they create environments where team members feel valued, supported, and empowered to bring their best selves to their roles.

Leaders can promote well-being by:

- **Modeling Self-Care:** Demonstrating healthy work-life balance and stress management techniques.
- **Providing Resources:** Offering access to wellness programs, mental health support, and flexible work arrangements.
- **Encouraging Open Dialogue:** Creating a culture where discussing mental health is accepted and encouraged.

Example: Arianna Huffington

- Arianna Huffington, founder of The Huffington Post and Thrive Global, has been a vocal advocate for workplace well-being. After experiencing burnout herself, she championed the importance of sleep, mindfulness, and self-care, influencing organizations worldwide to prioritize employee health.

An emotionally resilient leader encourages a culture that destigmatizes mental health concerns and fosters an atmosphere of open dialogue. This paves the way for team members to seek support and resources when needed, ultimately contributing to a healthier, more productive work environment.

Leading by Example

Emotionally resilient leaders set an example for others to follow. Their ability to remain positive and proactive encourages their teams to adopt similar attitudes.

Example: Jacinda Ardern

- Jacinda Ardern, the Prime Minister of New Zealand, is often cited for her emotional resilience, particularly in handling crises with empathy and decisiveness. Her leadership demonstrates how emotional resilience transcends borders and is a universal quality of effective leaders.

—

In the complex arena of leadership, emotional resilience emerges as a cornerstone, underpinning effective decision-making, inspiring confidence and trust, setting an example of adaptability, facilitating impactful communication, and promoting a culture of holistic well-being. It is not merely a desirable trait but an essential quality that distinguishes leaders who thrive in the face of adversity.

Emotional resilience empowers leaders to:

- **Navigate Challenges with Composure:** Maintaining effectiveness under pressure.
- **Make Judicious Decisions:** Balancing rational analysis with emotional awareness.
- **Foster Trust and Collaboration:** Building strong, cohesive teams.
- **Adapt to Change:** Embracing innovation and guiding others through transitions.
- **Support Well-Being:** Prioritizing the health and growth of team members.

As we delve deeper into the exploration of emotional resilience, we do so with the understanding that its significance in leadership is profound and far-reaching. By cultivating this essential quality, leaders can not only enhance their own effectiveness but also inspire and elevate those around them, driving collective success in an ever-changing world.

How Emotional Resilience Complements Other Leadership Skills

In the intricate tapestry of leadership, effective communication is the golden thread that binds teams together. Here, emotional resilience emerges as a critical enabler, enhancing a leader's ability to convey messages with precision, empathy, and unwavering confidence. While technical proficiency in communication is undoubtedly valuable, it is emotional resilience that infuses communication with the depth and authenticity required to resonate with team members.

Emotional resilience serves as a shield against the potential pitfalls of miscommunication. In emotionally charged or challenging situations, where tensions may run high, an emotionally resilient leader maintains their composure. This steadfastness allows them to navigate these encounters with grace and ensures that their messages are received with the intended clarity and impact.

Empathy, often regarded as the cornerstone of effective leadership, finds a natural ally in emotional resilience. Together, they form a formidable partnership that enables leaders to not only understand but also authentically connect with the emotions and perspectives of their team members. This empathetic resonance establishes a profound sense of trust and camaraderie within the team, fostering an environment where individuals feel seen, heard, and valued.

This combination of emotional resilience and empathy serves as a catalyst for creating a positive work culture. It engenders a sense of belonging and psychological safety, allowing team members to bring their authentic selves to their professional roles. In this inclusive environment, individuals are more likely to contribute their unique strengths and perspectives, ultimately leading to richer, more innovative outcomes.

Leadership, at its core, is about steering a collective effort towards a shared goal. In this context, emotional resilience emerges as an indispensable asset for navigating the complex landscape of team dynamics. Conflict, a natural byproduct of diverse perspectives and approaches, is met with equanimity by an emotionally resilient leader. Rather than shying away from challenges, they embrace them as opportunities for growth and learning.

Leaders with emotional resilience possess the acumen to foster a collaborative environment where each voice is not only heard but genuinely valued. They recognize that true innovation and effectiveness stem from the amalgamation of diverse viewpoints. This inclusivity, in turn, contributes to a culture of continuous improvement, where each team member is empowered to contribute their unique strengths and insights.

Effective leadership often hinges on the ability to make strategic decisions that propel the organization towards its goals. Here, emotional resilience plays a pivotal role in elevating the quality of decision-making. It ensures that leaders do not succumb to the pressures of the moment but instead approach decisions with a clear and discerning mind.

Emotional resilience introduces a critical dimension to the decision-making process – an understanding of the emotional implications of choices. A leader who is attuned to the emotional well-being of their team members can make decisions that not only drive organizational success but also prioritize the overall health and morale of the team.

Leadership is not solely about authority; it is about influence. An emotionally resilient leader possesses the capacity to inspire and motivate their team members, even in the face of adversity. This inspirational leadership style is not rooted in mere charisma, but in the authentic display of resilience in action.

When team members witness their leader navigating challenges with grace and determination, they are inspired to emulate this steadfastness in their own endeavors. This ripple effect, initiated by the leader's demonstration of emotional resilience, ultimately leads to a more engaged and motivated team.

In any collaborative endeavor, conflict is an inevitable companion. Here, emotional resilience emerges as a powerful tool for leaders to navigate and resolve conflicts effectively. It provides leaders with the ability to remain impartial and composed, even in emotionally charged situations.

Emotional resilience equips leaders with the discernment to identify underlying emotional triggers and address them with sensitivity and tact. This approach not only resolves the immediate conflict but also contributes to a healthier, more harmonious team dynamic.

In an era marked by rapid change and disruption, the ability to adapt is a non-negotiable trait for effective leaders.

Emotional resilience, with its emphasis on adaptability, aligns seamlessly with this requirement. Leaders who possess emotional resilience are not merely passive recipients of change; they are active champions of it.

They approach change with a growth-oriented mindset, viewing it as an opportunity for learning and development. This perspective, in turn, permeates the entire team, creating a culture that not only embraces change but thrives in it.

Effective delegation is a hallmark of successful leadership. It is not merely the distribution of tasks, but a strategic allocation of responsibilities that empowers team members to take ownership of their roles. Emotional resilience is instrumental in this process, as it enables leaders to entrust their team members with confidence.

An emotionally resilient leader recognizes that delegation is not a relinquishment of control, but a demonstration of trust in the capabilities of their team. This trust, reciprocated by team members, leads to increased morale, motivation, and ultimately, enhanced productivity.

Leadership, at its core, demands unwavering integrity and ethical conduct. Emotional resilience, by fostering inner strength and fortitude, supports leaders in upholding these principles, even in the face of moral dilemmas or external pressures.

In moments of ethical ambiguity, an emotionally resilient leader relies on their internal compass, guided by a steadfast commitment to doing what is right. This principled approach not only earns the respect and trust of team members but also sets a powerful example for the entire organization.

The demands of leadership are often multifaceted and relentless. Here, emotional resilience plays a critical role in enabling leaders to manage their time effectively and prioritize tasks with discernment. It ensures that leaders do not succumb to the tyranny of the urgent, but instead allocate their time in a manner that aligns with the organization's strategic objectives.

Emotional resilience provides leaders with the clarity and focus required to make informed decisions about where to invest their time and energy. This disciplined approach to time management ultimately leads to greater productivity and organizational success.

Leaders who possess emotional resilience recognize that learning is not confined to specific roles or hierarchies. Instead, it is a continuous, organization-wide endeavor. They foster a culture of learning that encourages team members to seek out new knowledge, take calculated risks, and view challenges as opportunities for growth.

This commitment to learning, driven by the leader's own display of emotional resilience, permeates the organization, creating an ecosystem that thrives on innovation and adaptability.

Innovation is the lifeblood of progress and growth. An emotionally resilient leader, unencumbered by fear of failure, is uniquely positioned to foster an environment of experimentation and creativity. They recognize that innovation often emerges from the willingness to take risks and the freedom to explore uncharted territories.

By providing a safe space for team members to innovate, an emotionally resilient leader unlocks the potential for groundbreaking ideas and solutions that can propel the organization forward.

In an era where customer-centricity is a defining factor of organizational success, emotional resilience proves invaluable. It enables leaders to approach customer interactions with empathy, understanding, and an unwavering commitment to providing value.

An emotionally resilient leader recognizes that each customer interaction is an opportunity to build trust and loyalty. They navigate these interactions with grace, ensuring that the customer feels heard and valued.

Inclusive leadership, which celebrates diversity and fosters an environment of equity and belonging, is critical in today's global landscape. Emotional resilience, with its emphasis on empathy and adaptability, aligns seamlessly with this imperative.

Leaders who possess emotional resilience are better equipped to understand and appreciate diverse perspectives. They recognize that diversity is not only a moral imperative but also a strategic advantage, leading to more innovative and effective outcomes.

In any collaborative endeavor, conflict is an inevitable companion. Here, emotional resilience emerges as a powerful tool for leaders to navigate and resolve conflicts effectively. It provides leaders with the ability to remain impartial and composed, even in emotionally charged situations.

Emotional resilience equips leaders with the discernment to identify underlying emotional triggers and address them with sensitivity and tact. This approach not only resolves the immediate conflict but also contributes to a healthier, more harmonious team dynamic.

In an era marked by rapid change and disruption, the ability to adapt is a non-negotiable trait for effective leaders. Emotional resilience, with its emphasis on adaptability, aligns seamlessly with this requirement. Leaders who possess emotional resilience are not merely passive recipients of change; they are active champions of it.

They approach change with a growth-oriented mindset, viewing it as an opportunity for learning and development. This perspective, in turn, permeates the entire team, creating a culture that not only embraces change but thrives in it.

Effective delegation is a hallmark of successful leadership. It is not merely the distribution of tasks, but a strategic allocation of responsibilities that empowers team members to take ownership of their roles. Emotional resilience is instrumental in this process, as it enables leaders to entrust their team members with confidence.

An emotionally resilient leader recognizes that delegation is not a relinquishment of control, but a demonstration of trust in the capabilities of their team. This trust, reciprocated by team members, leads to increased morale, motivation, and ultimately, enhanced productivity.

Leadership, at its core, demands unwavering integrity and ethical conduct. Emotional resilience, by fostering inner strength and fortitude, supports leaders in upholding these principles, even in the face of moral dilemmas or external pressures.

In moments of ethical ambiguity, an emotionally resilient leader relies on their internal compass, guided by a steadfast commitment to doing what is right. This principled approach not only earns the respect and trust of team members but also sets a powerful example for the entire organization.

The demands of leadership are often multifaceted and relentless. Here, emotional resilience plays a critical role in enabling leaders to manage their time effectively and prioritize tasks with discernment. It ensures that leaders do not succumb to the tyranny of the urgent, but instead allocate their time in a manner that aligns with the organization's strategic objectives.

Emotional resilience provides leaders with the clarity and focus required to make informed decisions about where to invest their time and energy. This disciplined approach to time management ultimately leads to greater productivity and organizational success.

Leaders who possess emotional resilience recognize that learning is not confined to specific roles or hierarchies. Instead, it is a continuous, organization-wide endeavor. They foster a culture of learning that encourages team members to seek out new knowledge, take calculated risks, and view challenges as opportunities for growth.

This commitment to learning, driven by the leader's own display of emotional resilience, permeates the organization, creating an ecosystem that thrives on innovation and adaptability.

Innovation is the lifeblood of progress and growth. An emotionally resilient leader, unencumbered by fear of failure, is uniquely positioned to foster an environment of experimentation and creativity. They recognize that innovation often emerges from the willingness to take risks and the freedom to explore uncharted territories.

By providing a safe space for team members to innovate, an emotionally resilient leader unlocks the potential for groundbreaking ideas and solutions that can propel the organization forward.

In an era where customer-centricity is a defining factor of organizational success, emotional resilience proves invaluable. It enables leaders to approach customer interactions with empathy, understanding, and an unwavering commitment to providing value.

An emotionally resilient leader recognizes that each customer interaction is an opportunity to build trust and loyalty. They navigate these interactions with grace, ensuring that the customer feels heard and valued.

Inclusive leadership, which celebrates diversity and fosters an environment of equity and belonging, is critical in today's global landscape. Emotional resilience, with its emphasis on empathy and adaptability, aligns seamlessly with this imperative.

Leaders who possess emotional resilience are better equipped to understand and appreciate diverse perspectives. They recognize that diversity is not only a moral imperative but also a strategic advantage, leading to more innovative and effective outcomes.

Communication is the bedrock of effective leadership, and its significance cannot be overstated. An emotionally resilient leader leverages this critical skill to forge strong connections with their team members. They communicate with clarity, empathy, and authenticity, ensuring that their messages resonate.

An emotionally resilient leader is attuned to the emotional undercurrents within the team. They possess the discernment to address sensitive topics with tact and navigate potentially challenging conversations with finesse. This ability to communicate effectively, even in emotionally charged situations, fosters an environment of trust and open dialogue.

Emotional resilience and emotional intelligence (EQ) are symbiotic forces that amplify a leader's effectiveness. While emotional intelligence provides the framework for understanding and managing emotions, emotional resilience infuses it with depth and fortitude.

An emotionally resilient leader exhibits a high degree of self-awareness, recognizing their own emotional responses and effectively managing them. This self-awareness not only enhances their own well-being but also sets the tone for the entire team, encouraging a culture of emotional intelligence.

Conflict, when navigated skillfully, has the potential to lead to innovation and growth. An emotionally resilient leader possesses the acumen to transform conflict from a disruptive force into a catalyst for positive change.

They approach conflict not with trepidation, but with a curiosity for the underlying issues and a commitment to finding mutually beneficial solutions. By fostering an environment where conflicts are addressed constructively, an emotionally resilient leader empowers their team to grow stronger in the face of challenges.

Effective decision-making is the crucible through which leadership is forged. An emotionally resilient leader approaches decisions with a clear mind and an unwavering commitment to the organization's vision.

In high-stakes situations, they do not waver under the weight of pressure. Instead, they draw upon their reservoir of emotional resilience to make informed, strategic decisions that steer the organization towards success.

Trust is the cornerstone of any successful team or organization. An emotionally resilient leader cultivates trust through their actions and their unwavering commitment to the team's well-being.

Team members are keenly attuned to the leader's emotional state and demeanor. When they witness a leader who handles challenges with grace and fortitude, it instills a sense of confidence and trust in their ability to navigate any situation.

Leadership presence is an intangible yet powerful quality that sets exceptional leaders apart. An emotionally resilient leader exudes a palpable sense of confidence and assurance, even in the face of uncertainty.

This presence, grounded in their inner strength and fortitude, commands respect and inspires confidence in the team. It creates a magnetic force that draws others towards the leader's vision and instills a sense of purpose and direction.

Innovation and progress often require a willingness to take calculated risks. An emotionally resilient leader approaches risk-taking with a balanced perspective, weighing the potential benefits against the possible pitfalls.

They are not driven by recklessness, but by a strategic understanding of the organization's goals and the calculated steps required to achieve them. This responsible approach to risk-taking sets the stage for meaningful growth and innovation.

True leadership is not about wielding power, but about empowering others to realize their full potential. An emotionally resilient leader recognizes the unique strengths and capabilities of each team member.

They create an environment where individuals feel supported and encouraged to take ownership of their roles. This empowerment, rooted in the leader's own display of emotional resilience, leads to a more engaged, motivated, and ultimately, high-performing team.

Organizations, like the individuals within them, must adapt and evolve to thrive in a dynamic landscape. An emotionally resilient leader serves as a beacon of stability and adaptability, guiding the organization through periods of change.

They approach change not as a disruptive force, but as an opportunity for growth and transformation. This perspective permeates the organization, creating a culture that embraces change as a natural and necessary part of progress.

Accountability is the linchpin that holds a high-performing team together. An emotionally resilient leader sets the standard for accountability through their own unwavering commitment to their responsibilities.

They do not shy away from challenges or difficult conversations, but face them head-on with a sense of purpose. This commitment to accountability sets the expectation for the entire team, ultimately leading to higher levels of performance and achievement.

Empathy, while a crucial leadership trait, must be balanced with the need for boundaries. An emotionally resilient leader navigates this delicate equilibrium with finesse.

They understand the importance of empathizing with team members' challenges while also maintaining clear expectations and standards. This balance fosters a supportive yet results-driven environment.

Conflict, when navigated skillfully, has the potential to lead to innovation and growth. An emotionally resilient leader possesses the acumen to transform conflict from a disruptive force into a catalyst for positive change.

They approach conflict not with trepidation, but with a curiosity for the underlying issues and a commitment to finding mutually beneficial solutions. By fostering an environment where conflicts are addressed constructively, an emotionally resilient leader empowers their team to grow stronger in the face of challenges.

Effective decision-making is the crucible through which leadership is forged. An emotionally resilient leader approaches decisions with a clear mind and an unwavering commitment to the organization's vision.

In high-stakes situations, they do not waver under the weight of pressure. Instead, they draw upon their reservoir of emotional resilience to make informed, strategic decisions that steer the organization towards success.

Trust is the cornerstone of any successful team or organization. An emotionally resilient leader cultivates trust through their actions and their unwavering commitment to the team's well-being.

Team members are keenly attuned to the leader's emotional state and demeanor. When they witness a leader who handles challenges with grace and fortitude, it instills a sense of confidence and trust in their ability to navigate any situation.

Leadership presence is an intangible yet powerful quality that sets exceptional leaders apart. An emotionally resilient leader exudes a palpable sense of confidence and assurance, even in the face of uncertainty.

This presence, grounded in their inner strength and fortitude, commands respect and inspires confidence in the team. It creates a magnetic force that draws others towards the leader's vision and instills a sense of purpose and direction.

Innovation and progress often require a willingness to take calculated risks. An emotionally resilient leader approaches risk-taking with a balanced perspective, weighing the potential benefits against the possible pitfalls.

They are not driven by recklessness, but by a strategic understanding of the organization's goals and the calculated steps required to achieve them. This responsible approach to risk-taking sets the stage for meaningful growth and innovation.

True leadership is not about wielding power, but about empowering others to realize their full potential. An emotionally resilient leader recognizes the unique strengths and capabilities of each team member.

They create an environment where individuals feel supported and encouraged to take ownership of their roles. This empowerment, rooted in the leader's own display of emotional resilience, leads to a more engaged, motivated, and ultimately, high-performing team.

Organizations, like the individuals within them, must adapt and evolve to thrive in a dynamic landscape. An emotionally resilient leader serves as a beacon of stability and adaptability, guiding the organization through periods of change.

They approach change not as a disruptive force, but as an opportunity for growth and transformation. This perspective permeates the organization, creating a culture that embraces change as a natural and necessary part of progress.

Accountability is the linchpin that holds a high-performing team together. An emotionally resilient leader sets the standard for accountability through their own unwavering commitment to their responsibilities.

They do not shy away from challenges or difficult conversations, but face them head-on with a sense of purpose. This commitment to accountability sets the expectation for the entire team, ultimately leading to higher levels of performance and achievement.

Empathy, while a crucial leadership trait, must be balanced with the need for boundaries. An emotionally resilient leader navigates this delicate equilibrium with finesse.

They understand the importance of empathizing with team members' challenges while also maintaining clear expectations and standards. This balance fosters a supportive yet results-driven environment.

Enhancing Effective Communication

Effective communication is the bedrock of successful leadership. Emotional resilience enriches this skill by allowing leaders to convey messages with clarity, empathy, and unwavering confidence—even in the most challenging situations. It enables leaders to:

- **Maintain Composure:** In emotionally charged scenarios, a resilient leader remains calm, preventing miscommunication that can arise from heightened emotions.
- **Express Authenticity:** Emotional resilience fosters authenticity, allowing leaders to communicate honestly while considering the emotional impact on their team.
- **Listen Actively:** Resilient leaders are better equipped to listen attentively, understanding both verbal and non-verbal cues, and responding appropriately.

Example: During a company-wide restructuring, a leader with emotional resilience can effectively communicate changes, address concerns empathetically, and maintain team morale.

Strengthening Empathy and Building Trust

Empathy is a cornerstone of effective leadership, and emotional resilience enhances a leader's capacity to genuinely understand and connect with team members. This synergy:

- **Builds Trust:** By showing genuine concern for team members' well-being, leaders foster a trusting environment.
- **Encourages Open Dialogue:** Teams are more likely to share ideas and concerns when they feel understood and supported.
- **Enhances Team Cohesion:** Empathy combined with resilience strengthens relationships, leading to a more unified team.

Example: A leader notices a team member struggling with workload. By empathetically addressing the issue and providing support, the leader not only assists the individual but also reinforces a supportive team culture.

Navigating Team Dynamics and Conflict Resolution

Conflict is an inevitable aspect of team dynamics. Emotional resilience equips leaders to:

- **Approach Conflict Constructively:** Viewing conflicts as opportunities for growth rather than threats.
- **Remain Impartial and Composed:** Managing personal emotions to facilitate fair and effective resolutions.
- **Foster Collaborative Solutions:** Encouraging team members to work together to find mutually beneficial outcomes.

Example: When two departments disagree on project priorities, an emotionally resilient leader can mediate discussions to find common ground.

Enhancing Decision-Making Abilities

High-stakes decisions often come with significant pressure. Emotional resilience aids leaders in:

- **Maintaining Clarity Under Pressure:** Keeping a clear mind to assess situations objectively.
- **Balancing Emotions and Logic:** Recognizing emotional biases that could affect decisions and mitigating them.
- **Confidence in Choices:** Standing by decisions despite challenges while remaining open to feedback.

Example: Facing a critical market shift, a resilient leader can make timely decisions to pivot strategies, balancing risks and opportunities.

Inspiring and Motivating Teams

Leadership is about influence and inspiration. Emotional resilience allows leaders to:

- **Model Resilience:** Demonstrating strength and adaptability inspires team members to adopt similar attitudes.
- **Maintain Optimism:** Keeping a positive outlook that motivates others, even during setbacks.
- **Encourage Perseverance:** Supporting team members through challenges fosters a culture of persistence.

Example: After a project setback, a resilient leader rallies the team to learn from mistakes and remain committed to goals.

Facilitating Adaptability and Embracing Change

In a rapidly changing world, adaptability is crucial. Emotional resilience enables leaders to:

- **Embrace Change Positively:** Viewing change as an opportunity rather than a threat.
- **Lead by Example:** Adapting behaviors and strategies encourages teams to follow suit.
- **Promote a Growth Mindset:** Encouraging continuous learning and flexibility among team members.

Example: Implementing new technologies, a resilient leader guides the team through the transition, addressing fears and highlighting benefits.

Empowering Through Effective Delegation

Delegation is more than assigning tasks; it's about empowering others. Emotional resilience helps leaders:

- **Trust Team Members:** Confidently delegate responsibilities, trusting in their team's capabilities.
- **Develop Others:** Provide opportunities for growth and skill development.
- **Prevent Burnout:** By sharing the workload, leaders maintain their own well-being and model work-life balance.

Example: Delegating leadership of a project to a team member, a resilient leader provides support while encouraging autonomy.

Upholding Integrity and Ethical Leadership

Emotional resilience supports leaders in maintaining ethical standards, even when challenged:

- **Resist External Pressures:** Standing firm against unethical practices despite pressures.
- **Lead with Principles:** Making decisions aligned with core values.
- **Build Organizational Integrity:** Setting a tone of honesty and accountability.

Example: Refusing to compromise product quality for cost savings, a leader reinforces the company's commitment to excellence.

Enhancing Time Management and Prioritization

With numerous demands, leaders need to manage time effectively. Emotional resilience aids in:

- **Staying Focused:** Avoiding distractions from stress or emotional turmoil.
- **Prioritizing Tasks:** Assessing what is most important for achieving goals.
- **Maintaining Energy Levels:** Managing stress to prevent fatigue and maintain productivity.

Example: During a crisis, a resilient leader prioritizes critical issues without becoming overwhelmed by less urgent tasks.

Fostering a Culture of Learning and Innovation

Emotional resilience encourages a learning environment by:

- **Embracing Failures as Learning Opportunities:** Viewing setbacks as valuable lessons.
- **Encouraging Experimentation:** Supporting creative thinking and risk-taking.
- **Continuous Self-Improvement:** Modeling a commitment to personal growth.

Example: After a failed product launch, the leader initiates a debrief to extract learnings and encourages innovative solutions.

Enhancing Customer Relationships

Customer-centricity is vital for success. Emotional resilience helps leaders:

- **Handle Customer Feedback Gracefully:** Managing emotions when receiving criticism.
- **Build Strong Relationships:** Connecting authentically with customers to understand their needs.
- **Maintain Professionalism:** Providing excellent service even under challenging circumstances.

Example: Addressing a customer's complaint, a resilient leader listens empathetically and works toward a satisfactory resolution.

Promoting Inclusive Leadership

Emotional resilience supports inclusive practices by:

- **Valuing Diversity:** Recognizing and appreciating different perspectives.
- **Adapting Communication Styles:** Adjusting approaches to meet diverse team needs.
- **Challenging Biases:** Reflecting on personal biases and promoting equity.

Example: Facilitating a diverse team's collaboration by ensuring all voices are heard and respected.

Strengthening Leadership Presence

Leadership presence is an intangible quality that commands respect. Emotional resilience contributes by:

- **Projecting Confidence:** Remaining self-assured even in uncertain times.
- **Demonstrating Composure:** Handling stress visibly well, which reassures others.
- **Exuding Authenticity:** Being genuine builds credibility and trust.

Example: During a major organizational change, the leader's composed demeanor instills confidence in the team's ability to navigate the transition.

Enabling Responsible Risk-Taking

Innovation often requires taking risks. Emotional resilience allows leaders to:

- **Assess Risks Objectively:** Balancing potential gains against possible losses without emotional bias.
- **Overcome Fear of Failure:** Not letting fear inhibit progress.
- **Learn from Outcomes:** Whether successful or not, extracting lessons from risk-taking endeavors.

Example: Investing in a new market, the leader carefully evaluates the opportunity and leads the team with confidence.

Empowering Others

An emotionally resilient leader empowers team members by:

- **Delegating Authority:** Allowing others to make decisions and take ownership.
- **Providing Support:** Offering resources and guidance as needed.
- **Recognizing Achievements:** Celebrating successes to motivate and encourage.

Example: Acknowledging a team member's innovative idea and providing support to develop it further.

Promoting Accountability

Emotional resilience fosters a culture of accountability by:

- **Setting Clear Expectations:** Communicating roles and responsibilities transparently.
- **Holding Oneself Accountable:** Leading by example in meeting commitments.
- **Addressing Issues Directly:** Confronting problems constructively without avoiding difficult conversations.

Example: When a project misses a deadline, the leader works with the team to understand causes and implement solutions.

Balancing Empathy with Boundaries

While empathy is crucial, leaders must also maintain professional boundaries. Emotional resilience helps in:

- **Avoiding Emotional Overload:** Managing one's own emotions to stay effective.
- **Establishing Limits:** Knowing when to say no or delegate tasks.
- **Maintaining Objectivity:** Supporting others without becoming enmeshed in their emotional states.

Example: Supporting a team member through personal challenges while ensuring project goals remain on track.

—

Emotional resilience is not just an addition to a leader's skill set but a powerful enhancer that complements and strengthens other leadership abilities. By integrating emotional resilience into their leadership approach, leaders can communicate more effectively, build stronger relationships, navigate challenges adeptly, and foster a positive, productive organizational culture. In doing so, they not only elevate their own performance but also inspire and empower those around them to achieve collective success.

The Impact of Emotional Resilience on Leadership Effectiveness

In the crucible of leadership, decisions made under pressure can have far-reaching consequences. An emotionally resilient leader possesses the capacity to navigate high-stakes situations with clarity and composure. This heightened emotional state allows for a more balanced perspective, ensuring that decisions are not driven by panic or short-term considerations, but rather grounded in a clear understanding of the organization's long-term objectives. Through their resilient approach, leaders instill confidence in their teams, demonstrating that even in the most challenging circumstances, rational and strategic decision-making is achievable.

A leader's emotional state and demeanor have a profound impact on the motivation and productivity of their team. An emotionally resilient leader sets the tone by exhibiting a proactive, can-do attitude even in the face of obstacles. This positivity is contagious, inspiring team members to approach their tasks with a similar sense of determination and resolve. Additionally, an emotionally resilient leader recognizes the individual strengths and contributions of team members, providing constructive feedback and recognition. This fosters a sense of purpose and belonging, ultimately leading to higher levels of motivation and productivity.

The work culture cultivated by a leader significantly influences the overall atmosphere of the organization. An emotionally resilient leader fosters an environment where challenges are viewed as opportunities for growth, rather than insurmountable obstacles. This perspective permeates the organization, creating a culture of resilience and adaptability. Furthermore, an emotionally resilient leader leads by example, demonstrating the importance of self-care and well-being. By prioritizing their own emotional health, they set the expectation that all team members should do the same. This focus on holistic well-being contributes to a positive and supportive work atmosphere.

Boosting Team Motivation and Productivity

A leader's emotional state significantly influences their team's motivation and productivity. Emotionally resilient leaders positively impact their teams by:

- **Setting a Positive Tone:** Exhibiting a proactive, optimistic attitude that inspires team members to adopt a similar mindset.
- **Recognizing Individual Contributions:** Providing constructive feedback and acknowledging achievements fosters a sense of value and purpose among team members.
- **Modeling Resilience:** Demonstrating the ability to bounce back from setbacks encourages others to do the same.

Example: Satya Nadella, CEO of Microsoft, transformed the company's culture by promoting growth mindset principles. His emphasis on learning from failures and his resilient outlook energized employees, leading to increased innovation and collaboration.

This contagious positivity motivates team members to tackle challenges with enthusiasm, enhancing overall productivity and engagement.

Cultivating a Resilient Organizational Culture

The culture established by leadership profoundly affects the organization's atmosphere and effectiveness. Emotionally resilient leaders contribute to building a culture that:

- **Embraces Challenges:** Viewing obstacles as opportunities for growth rather than threats.
- **Encourages Adaptability:** Promoting flexibility and openness to change at all organizational levels.
- **Prioritizes Well-being:** Recognizing the importance of mental, emotional, and physical health in sustaining high performance.

By leading through example, such leaders:

- **Demonstrate Self-Care:** Prioritize their well-being, signaling to employees that it's acceptable and important to do the same.
- **Support Work-Life Balance:** Implement policies and practices that allow employees to maintain a healthy balance between professional and personal life.
- **Foster Psychological Safety:** Create an environment where employees feel safe to express ideas, take risks, and voice concerns without fear of negative consequences.

Example: Airbnb CEO Brian Chesky emphasizes a culture of belonging and support. During the COVID-19 pandemic, despite having to make difficult decisions, he communicated transparently and compassionately, maintaining trust and commitment within the organization.

Promoting Innovation and Creativity

Emotional resilience equips leaders to foster an environment where innovation thrives:

- **Encouraging Experimentation:** Resilient leaders are open to new ideas and understand that failure is part of the innovation process.
- **Learning from Setbacks:** They model how to extract valuable lessons from unsuccessful endeavors.
- **Supporting Creative Thinking:** By managing stress and maintaining a positive outlook, they create space for creativity to flourish.

Example: Sir Richard Branson, the founder of the Virgin Group, exemplifies emotional resilience through his ability to learn from setbacks. Branson's leadership style is characterized by a strong emphasis on creativity and innovation. By maintaining a positive outlook and managing stress effectively, he fosters a corporate culture that encourages bold ideas and entrepreneurial thinking. At Virgin, employees are empowered to think outside the box and challenge conventional wisdom. Branson believes that providing a supportive environment where team members can explore new concepts without fear of failure is key to driving innovation.

Strengthening Relationships with Stakeholders

Emotionally resilient leaders are better equipped to build and maintain strong relationships with customers, investors, and partners:

- **Effective Communication:** They convey messages clearly and empathetically, even during challenging times.
- **Conflict Resolution:** Resilience aids in navigating disagreements constructively, preserving important relationships.
- **Trust Building:** Consistent, composed leadership enhances credibility and trustworthiness.

Example: Mary Barra, CEO of General Motors, faced significant challenges with product recalls. Her transparent communication and commitment to addressing issues head-on helped rebuild trust with customers and regulators.

Enhancing Personal Well-being and Sustainable Leadership

Leadership roles are inherently demanding. Emotional resilience supports leaders in sustaining their effectiveness over time by:

- **Preventing Burnout:** Managing stress and practicing self-care techniques to maintain health and vitality.
- **Balancing Priorities:** Recognizing the importance of personal life and setting boundaries to ensure long-term sustainability.
- **Continuous Growth:** Embracing lifelong learning and personal development.

Example: Leaders like Arianna Huffington have emphasized the importance of well-being. After experiencing burnout, she founded Thrive Global to promote health and productivity, highlighting how personal resilience can lead to broader positive impacts.

Fostering Team Cohesion and Collaboration

Emotionally resilient leaders strengthen team dynamics by:

- **Building Trust:** Their consistent and reliable behavior fosters trust among team members.
- **Facilitating Open Communication:** They encourage dialogue, ensuring that team members feel heard and valued.
- **Resolving Conflicts:** By approaching conflicts with composure, they can mediate effectively and find collaborative solutions.

Example: Tim Cook, CEO of Apple, is known for his approachable leadership style. His emotional resilience has helped maintain Apple's collaborative culture, encouraging innovation through teamwork.

Adapting to Change and Uncertainty

In an era of rapid change, leaders must guide their organizations through uncertainty:

- **Embracing Change:** Resilient leaders view change as an opportunity rather than a threat.
- **Guiding Others:** They provide support and direction, helping team members navigate transitions.

- **Maintaining Stability:** Their steady presence reduces anxiety and keeps teams focused.

Example: Ginni Rometty, former CEO of IBM, led the company through significant shifts towards cloud computing and AI. Her resilient leadership helped the organization adapt to new technological landscapes.

Emotional resilience is a cornerstone of effective leadership. Its impact extends beyond individual well-being, influencing decision-making, team motivation, organizational culture, innovation, stakeholder relationships, and adaptability. By cultivating emotional resilience, leaders can navigate the complexities of modern business with confidence and integrity, inspiring their teams to achieve collective success.

Investing in developing emotional resilience is not just beneficial—it's essential. Organizations that support their leaders and employees in building this resilience position themselves to thrive amid challenges and emerge stronger in the face of adversity.

Improved Decision-Making under Pressure

Leadership often operates in an environment where decisions must be made swiftly, often in the midst of uncertainty and intense pressure. Here, emotional resilience emerges as an invaluable asset. It equips leaders with the mental fortitude needed to make sound decisions, even when the stakes are at their highest.

In such critical moments, emotions can run high, clouding judgment and leading to impulsive choices. An emotionally resilient leader, however, possesses the ability to remain composed. They acknowledge the intensity of the situation without succumbing to it. This capacity to navigate through high-stress scenarios with clarity is instrumental in ensuring that decisions are not merely reactive, but rather carefully considered.

Emotional resilience enables leaders to maintain a long-term perspective. They understand that decisions made in the heat of the moment can have far-reaching consequences, both for the organization and its members. This broader view allows them to weigh the immediate needs against the strategic goals and values of the organization. They steer away from shortsighted choices driven by fear or urgency, opting instead for a path that aligns with the organization's overall vision.

In essence, an emotionally resilient leader serves as a beacon of stability in turbulent times. Their equipoise reassures team members, instilling confidence in the decision-making process. It sends a powerful message that even in the most challenging circumstances, rational and strategic choices are not only possible but expected. This confidence permeates the organization, creating an environment where individuals can trust in the leadership's ability to steer the ship, even through the stormiest of waters.

The impact of improved decision-making under pressure extends beyond immediate outcomes. It influences the organization's overall trajectory, ensuring that it remains on course towards its strategic objectives. It builds a reputation for level-headedness and reliability, qualities that are highly valued not only by team members but also by stakeholders and partners.

In times of crisis, the decisions made by leaders become the North Star that guides the organization. Through emotional resilience, leaders forge a path that is not swayed by momentary turbulence but is anchored in a steadfast commitment to the organization's mission and values. It is this unwavering resolve that distinguishes exceptional leadership from the rest, and it is this very resolve that emotional resilience fortifies.

Enhancing Decision-Making Under Pressure

Leaders are often required to make pivotal decisions in the face of uncertainty, tight deadlines, and high stakes. Emotional resilience plays a vital role in enhancing their decision-making capabilities by:

- **Maintaining Composure:** Resilient leaders remain calm under pressure, which allows them to process information more effectively and avoid rash judgments.
- **Strategic Thinking:** They can focus on the bigger picture, ensuring that immediate decisions align with long-term goals and organizational vision.

- **Balancing Emotions and Logic:** Emotional resilience enables leaders to recognize and regulate their emotions, preventing fear or anxiety from clouding their judgment.

Example: During the 2008 financial crisis, Alan Mulally, then-CEO of Ford Motor Company, demonstrated emotional resilience by making tough decisions to restructure the company without accepting a government bailout. His steady leadership and strategic focus helped Ford navigate the crisis successfully.

Through their resilient approach, leaders instill confidence in their teams and stakeholders, signaling that challenges can be overcome with thoughtful action rather than panic.

Maintaining Composure

Emotionally resilient leaders remain calm under pressure, which allows them to:

- **Process Information Effectively:** A calm mind can assimilate and analyze information more thoroughly, leading to better-informed decisions.
- **Avoid Rash Judgments:** By not succumbing to panic or stress, they prevent hasty decisions that may lead to negative outcomes.
- **Project Confidence:** Their composure reassures team members and stakeholders, fostering trust and stability within the organization.

Example: Lee Kuan Yew

- As the founding Prime Minister of Singapore, Lee Kuan Yew faced immense challenges in transforming a small, resource-poor nation into a thriving global city-state. In 1965, when Singapore was unexpectedly expelled from Malaysia, Lee Kuan Yew confronted a crisis that threatened the nation's survival. Despite the emotional weight of the situation—evident in his tearful announcement of the separation—he quickly regained composure. His emotional resilience allowed him to focus on strategic initiatives such as building a robust economy, establishing strong international relationships, and promoting social cohesion. His ability to remain calm under intense pressure was instrumental in laying the foundation for Singapore's success.

Through their resilient approach, leaders instill confidence in their teams and stakeholders, signaling that challenges can be overcome with thoughtful action rather than panic.

Strategic Thinking

Emotionally resilient leaders can focus on the bigger picture, ensuring that immediate decisions align with long-term goals and organizational vision.

Example: Tsai Ing-wen

- As the President of Taiwan, Tsai Ing-wen has faced significant pressure from both domestic and international fronts, particularly regarding Taiwan's relationship with mainland China. During the COVID-19 pandemic, Tsai demonstrated strategic thinking by implementing swift public health measures, including early travel restrictions and widespread mask distribution. Despite initial skepticism and economic concerns, her decisions prioritized public health over short-term economic gains. Taiwan's effective control of the virus not only saved lives but also positioned its economy for a quicker recovery. Tsai's emotional resilience enabled her to balance immediate pressures with long-term national well-being.

Balancing Emotions and Logic

Emotional resilience enables leaders to recognize and regulate their emotions, preventing fear or anxiety from clouding their judgment.

Example: Shinzo Abe

- As Japan's longest-serving Prime Minister, Shinzo Abe faced multiple challenges, including economic stagnation, natural disasters, and geopolitical tensions. In response to Japan's prolonged economic issues, Abe introduced "Abenomics," a bold economic strategy comprising monetary easing, fiscal stimulus, and structural reforms. Implementing these policies required balancing public concern over national debt and skepticism about unorthodox methods. Abe's emotional resilience allowed him to manage public criticisms and focus on data-driven decisions aimed at revitalizing Japan's economy. His ability to balance emotions and logic was crucial in pursuing policies that sought long-term economic growth.

Case Study: Narendra Modi

Maintaining Composure and Strategic Thinking

- As the Prime Minister of India, Narendra Modi has faced numerous high-pressure situations requiring decisive action. One notable example is the 2016 demonetization initiative, where high-denomination currency notes were invalidated overnight to combat corruption and illicit financial activities. Despite the massive disruption this caused in the short term, including public inconvenience and economic slowdown, Modi maintained composure in the face of widespread criticism. He communicated the long-term benefits of the policy, emphasizing goals like reducing corruption and promoting a digital economy. His emotional resilience allowed him to stay focused on strategic objectives, balancing immediate challenges with envisioned future benefits for India's economy.

Balancing Emotions and Logic

- During the COVID-19 pandemic, Modi had to make critical decisions balancing public health concerns with economic implications in a nation of over a billion people. Implementing one of the world's largest lockdowns, he addressed the nation with empathy, acknowledging the hardships while explaining the necessity of stringent measures. His emotional resilience enabled him to regulate both his own emotions and those of the public, ensuring actions were strategic and aimed at safeguarding the population.

Instilling Confidence Through Resilient Leadership

Through their resilient approach, leaders instill confidence in their teams and stakeholders by:

- **Demonstrating Reliability:** Consistent behavior under pressure reassures others of the leader's stability.
- **Encouraging Trust:** Teams are more likely to trust leaders who handle stress effectively and make thoughtful decisions.

- **Fostering a Positive Environment:** A leader's resilience can uplift morale and motivate others to perform at their best.

Example: Dr. Tedros Adhanom Ghebreyesus

- As the Director-General of the World Health Organization (WHO), Dr. Tedros Adhanom Ghebreyesus has worked closely with Asian nations during global health crises. During the COVID-19 pandemic, he demonstrated emotional resilience by providing consistent leadership amidst criticism and immense pressure. His calm demeanor and commitment to data-driven strategies helped coordinate international responses. By balancing emotions and logic, he aimed to instill confidence among member countries, including those in Asia, promoting collaboration and effective action against the pandemic.

Enhancing decision-making under pressure is a critical aspect of leadership effectiveness. Emotional resilience empowers leaders to maintain composure, think strategically, and balance emotions with logic, even in the most challenging circumstances. By cultivating these abilities, leaders not only make better decisions but also inspire confidence and trust among their teams and stakeholders.

Through thoughtful action rather than panic, resilient leaders navigate their organizations toward success, turning obstacles into opportunities for growth. As demonstrated by leaders like Lee Kuan Yew, Tsai Ing-wen, Shinzo Abe, Narendra Modi, and others, emotional resilience is a powerful asset that enhances leadership effectiveness and drives positive outcomes in the face of adversity.

Enhancing Team Motivation and Productivity

Leaders serve as the emotional barometer of a team or organization. Their The emotional state of a leader acts as a powerful barometer for the entire team or organization. An emotionally resilient leader doesn't just manage their own emotions effectively; they set the tone for the group's collective mindset. Their demeanor, attitude, and approach to challenges profoundly influence team motivation and productivity. By cultivating emotional resilience, leaders become catalysts for creating high-functioning, motivated, and cohesive teams.

The Leader as an Emotional Anchor

An emotionally resilient leader serves as a steady anchor amidst the turbulent seas of organizational challenges. Just as a lighthouse provides guidance and reassurance to ships navigating stormy waters, such leaders offer stability and direction to their teams during times of uncertainty. Their unwavering positivity and proactive attitude send a powerful, reassuring message: challenges are surmountable, and setbacks are temporary. This optimism is not naive but grounded in a realistic assessment of situations coupled with a firm belief in the team's capabilities.

Example: Consider a project manager who, upon learning that a critical deadline has been moved up, maintains composure and communicates a clear action plan to the team. Instead of expressing panic or frustration, they focus on solutions, which in turn encourages the team to rally and meet the new deadline.

The Contagious Nature of Resilience

Emotional resilience is inherently contagious. When leaders consistently demonstrate confidence, determination, and a positive outlook, these attitudes permeate the team. Team members are more likely to adopt similar behaviors, approaching their tasks with increased enthusiasm and commitment. This phenomenon is supported by the concept of emotional contagion in organizational psychology, where emotions and attitudes can spread throughout a group, influencing overall morale and performance.

Research Insight: Studies have shown that leaders' emotional expressions can significantly impact team members' moods and job satisfaction. A leader's positive emotions can enhance creativity, cooperation, and overall productivity within the team.

Recognizing and Valuing Individual Contributions

Emotionally resilient leaders understand the profound impact of acknowledging and valuing each team member's contributions. They take the time to provide constructive feedback, celebrate successes, and recognize efforts, no matter how small. This practice fosters a sense of purpose and belonging among team members, which is crucial for maintaining high levels of motivation and engagement.

- **Constructive Feedback:** Offering specific, actionable insights helps team members grow and improves performance.
- **Celebrating Achievements:** Publicly recognizing accomplishments boosts morale and reinforces desired behaviors.
- **Personal Acknowledgment:** Taking the time to understand and appreciate individual strengths and aspirations strengthens the leader-team member relationship.

Example: A leader who notices an employee's extra effort to meet a client's needs might send a personalized note of appreciation or acknowledge them during a team meeting, reinforcing their value to the organization.

Creating a Psychologically Safe Environment

Emotional resilience contributes to building a psychologically safe workplace where team members feel comfortable expressing their ideas, concerns, and mistakes without fear of ridicule or retribution. This openness encourages innovation, as employees are more willing to take calculated risks and share creative solutions.

- **Encouraging Open Dialogue:** Leaders invite input and actively listen to diverse perspectives.
- **Embracing Mistakes as Learning Opportunities:** Viewing errors as part of the growth process reduces fear of failure.
- **Fostering Mutual Respect:** Establishing norms of respect and support enhances collaboration.

Impact on Productivity: When team members feel safe and supported, they are more likely to go above and beyond in their roles, leading to increased productivity and better outcomes.

The Negative Impact of Lacking Emotional Resilience

Conversely, leaders who lack emotional resilience may inadvertently create an environment of uncertainty and stress. Signs include:

- **Inconsistent Reactions:** Unpredictable emotional responses can confuse and unsettle team members.
- **Negative Attitudes:** Pessimism or defeatism from leadership can demotivate the team.
- **Failure to Acknowledge Contributions:** Overlooking team efforts leads to disengagement and diminished morale.

Consequences: Such environments can result in higher turnover rates, reduced job satisfaction, and lower productivity, ultimately affecting the organization's success.

Case Study: Emotional Resilience in Action

Scenario: During an unexpected economic downturn, a company's sales plummet, leading to widespread concern about job security among employees.

Leader's Response:
- **Communication:** The leader holds an open forum to address concerns, providing transparent information about the company's situation and plans.

- **Positivity and Assurance:** They express confidence in the team's ability to navigate the crisis together, emphasizing collective strengths.
- **Action Plan:** A clear strategy is outlined, involving team input to foster ownership and commitment.

Outcome: The team's morale stabilizes, and they focus on innovative ways to improve sales, ultimately helping the company recover more quickly than anticipated.

—

Emotional resilience is a cornerstone of effective leadership that significantly impacts team motivation and productivity. By embodying resilience, leaders inspire their teams to adopt a positive, proactive approach to challenges. Recognizing individual contributions, fostering psychological safety, and maintaining a steady, optimistic demeanor are key practices that elevate team performance. Conversely, a lack of emotional resilience can lead to disengagement and decreased productivity. Therefore, investing in developing emotional resilience is not only beneficial for leaders personally but is also crucial for cultivating motivated, high-performing teams that drive organizational success.

Creating a Positive Work Culture and Atmosphere:

The culture within an organization is a mirror reflecting its leadership's values, behaviors, and attitudes. Emotional resilience in leadership acts as a powerful catalyst for cultivating a positive, growth-oriented work environment. Leaders who embody emotional resilience understand that challenges are not insurmountable roadblocks but opportunities for learning, development, and innovation. This perspective permeates the organization, fostering a culture characterized by resilience, adaptability, and continuous improvement.

In a culture of emotional resilience, setbacks are not met with defeat, but with a collective determination to find solutions and forge ahead. This outlook encourages team members to approach challenges with creativity, innovation, and a forward-looking mindset. Instead of dwelling on failures, they view them as stepping stones toward progress.

An emotionally resilient leader leads by example when it comes to prioritizing well-being and self-care. They recognize that a healthy work-life balance is not a luxury but a necessity for sustained success. By openly valuing their own emotional health, they set the expectation that all team members should do the same. This not only fosters a culture of self-care but also reduces the stigma around mental health, creating a safe space for open discussions and support.

An emotionally resilient leader promotes a sense of belonging and inclusivity. They celebrate diversity and encourage a multiplicity of perspectives. This inclusivity not only enriches the work environment but also enhances problem-solving and creativity. When individuals from different backgrounds and experiences come together, the potential for innovation and growth is limitless.

In contrast, a leader who lacks emotional resilience may inadvertently cultivate a culture of fear or avoidance. Challenges may be met with trepidation, and failures may be swept under the rug. This can create an atmosphere of stagnation and hinder the organization's ability to adapt to change.

A leader who neglects their own well-being sets a dangerous precedent. Team members may feel compelled to overwork or ignore their own emotional health in an attempt to emulate their leader. This can lead to burnout, decreased morale, and ultimately, reduced productivity.

Not only does emotional resilience serve as the cornerstone of a positive work culture and atmosphere, but it also instills a growth-oriented perspective, encourages self-care, and promotes inclusivity. Through their actions and attitudes, emotionally resilient leaders create an environment where challenges are met with courage, setbacks are viewed as opportunities, and individuals are supported in their holistic well-being. This, in turn, leads to a thriving organizational culture characterized by adaptability, creativity, and a shared commitment to excellence.

Fostering a Growth Mindset

An emotionally resilient leader instills a growth mindset within the team—a belief that abilities and intelligence can be developed through dedication and hard work. This mindset transforms setbacks into stepping stones rather than stumbling blocks. When challenges arise, the team collectively approaches them with determination, creativity, and optimism. This proactive attitude encourages:

- **Innovation:** Team members feel empowered to experiment and take calculated risks without fear of undue criticism or failure.
- **Collaboration:** A shared commitment to overcoming obstacles fosters stronger teamwork and open communication.
- **Continuous Learning:** Embracing challenges as learning opportunities promotes personal and professional development.

Example: Satya Nadella, CEO of Microsoft, revitalized the company's culture by promoting a growth mindset. Under his leadership, Microsoft shifted from a fixed mindset culture, where employees were hesitant to share ideas for fear of failure, to one where learning from mistakes is valued. This change led to increased collaboration, innovation, and a resurgence in the company's performance.

Prioritizing Well-Being and Self-Care

Emotionally resilient leaders recognize that employee well-being is not just a personal matter but a strategic organizational priority. By prioritizing their own well-being and modeling healthy work-life balance, leaders set a precedent for the entire organization. This approach:

- **Reduces Burnout:** Encouraging self-care helps prevent physical and emotional exhaustion among employees.
- **Enhances Productivity:** Well-rested and healthy employees are more focused, creative, and efficient.
- **Builds Trust:** Demonstrating concern for employees' well-being fosters loyalty and engagement.

Strategies for Leaders:

- **Promote Flexible Work Arrangements:** Offer options like remote work or flexible hours to accommodate personal needs.
- **Encourage Time Off:** Support employees in taking vacations and breaks to recharge.
- **Provide Resources:** Implement wellness programs, mental health support, and stress management workshops.

Example: Arianna Huffington, founder of Thrive Global, champions the importance of well-being in the workplace. After experiencing burnout herself, she has advocated for organizational practices that prioritize sleep, mindfulness, and self-care, emphasizing that these factors are crucial for sustained success.

Cultivating Inclusivity and Diversity

An emotionally resilient leader understands that diversity and inclusivity are strengths that enrich the organizational environment. By celebrating diverse perspectives and backgrounds, leaders can enhance problem-solving and creativity within the team. This inclusivity:

- **Encourages Different Perspectives:** Diverse teams bring varied experiences and ideas, leading to more innovative solutions.
- **Improves Employee Engagement:** When individuals feel valued for their unique contributions, they are more committed and motivated.
- **Strengthens Organizational Reputation:** A commitment to diversity can enhance the organization's image and attract top talent.

Strategies for Leaders:

Implement Inclusive Hiring Practices: Actively seek candidates from various backgrounds.

Promote Open Dialogue: Create forums where all employees feel comfortable sharing ideas and feedback.

Provide Diversity Training: Educate teams on the value of inclusivity and how to practice it daily.

Example: Indra Nooyi, former CEO of PepsiCo, emphasized diversity and inclusion as key components of the company's strategy. She fostered a culture where different viewpoints were encouraged, leading to innovative products and global market expansion.

Leading by Example

Emotional resilience in leadership is most impactful when leaders lead by example. Their actions and attitudes set the tone for the entire organization. By openly demonstrating resilience, adaptability, and a positive outlook, leaders inspire their teams to adopt similar behaviors.

- **Transparency:** Sharing both successes and challenges authentically builds trust.
- **Accountability:** Owning mistakes and learning from them encourages a culture of continuous improvement.
- **Optimism:** Maintaining a positive attitude, even during tough times, motivates others to persevere.

Example: Jacinda Ardern, Prime Minister of New Zealand, has been praised for her compassionate and resilient leadership, particularly during crises such as the Christchurch mosque shootings and the COVID-19 pandemic. Her empathetic and decisive actions have unified the nation and fostered a culture of kindness and collective responsibility.

Building Psychological Safety

Creating a positive work culture involves establishing psychological safety, where team members feel safe to take risks and express themselves without fear of negative consequences. Emotionally resilient leaders promote this environment by:

- **Encouraging Open Communication:** Actively listening to employees and valuing their input.

- **Supporting Risk-Taking:** Rewarding innovative ideas, even if they don't always succeed.
- **Addressing Issues Constructively:** Focusing on solutions rather than assigning blame.

Benefits of Psychological Safety:

- **Increased Engagement:** Employees are more invested when they feel their contributions matter.
- **Enhanced Learning:** Mistakes are seen as learning opportunities, leading to growth and development.
- **Better Performance:** Teams that communicate openly can collaborate more effectively and adapt quickly to changes.
- **Research Insight:** A study by Google's Project Aristotle found that psychological safety is the most important factor in high-performing teams.

Avoiding Negative Cultural Impacts

Leaders who lack emotional resilience may inadvertently create a culture of fear, stagnation, or burnout:

- **Fear of Failure:** If mistakes are punished harshly, employees may avoid taking necessary risks, hindering innovation.
- **Overwork Culture:** Leaders who neglect their own well-being may set unrealistic expectations, leading to employee burnout.
- **Resistance to Change:** A lack of adaptability can cause organizations to fall behind in a rapidly evolving market.

Example: Organizations with high-pressure, fear-driven cultures often experience high turnover rates, low employee satisfaction, and reduced productivity.

Emotional resilience is the cornerstone of a positive work culture and atmosphere. By fostering a growth-oriented perspective, encouraging self-care, promoting inclusivity, and leading by example, emotionally resilient leaders create environments where challenges are met with courage and optimism. Employees feel supported in their holistic well-being, leading to increased adaptability, creativity, and a shared commitment to excellence.

In such cultures, organizations are better equipped to navigate the complexities of today's business landscape, retain top talent, and achieve sustained success. Emotional resilience doesn't just benefit individual leaders—it transforms entire organizations into resilient, thriving entities ready to face any challenge.

Strategies for Leaders to Enhance Emotional Resilience

1. Self-Awareness and Reflection:

- Regularly assess your emotional responses and their impact on others.
- Practice mindfulness to stay present and manage stress effectively.

2. Developing Emotional Intelligence:

- Work on recognizing and understanding your own emotions and those of others.
- Use empathy to connect with team members on a deeper level.

3. Positive Mindset Cultivation:
- Focus on solutions rather than dwelling on problems.
- Encourage optimism within the team by highlighting successes and progress.

4. Building Strong Relationships:
- Invest time in getting to know your team members personally.
- Establish trust through consistent, honest communication.

5. Stress Management Techniques:
- Engage in activities that reduce stress, such as exercise, hobbies, or meditation.
- Encourage work-life balance for yourself and your team.

6. Continuous Learning and Development:
- Seek feedback on your leadership style and be open to change.
- Attend workshops or coaching sessions focused on building resilience and leadership skills.

Implementing these strategies not only enhances a leader's emotional resilience but also sets a powerful example for team members to follow.

Strategies to Cultivate Emotional Resilience in Organizations

Leaders can actively cultivate emotional resilience within their organizations by:

1. Providing Training and Development:

- **Resilience Workshops:** Offer programs that teach coping strategies and stress management.
- **Leadership Development:** Encourage leaders at all levels to develop emotional intelligence and resilience skills.

2. Recognizing and Rewarding Resilience:

- **Celebrate Successes:** Acknowledge not just outcomes but the effort and perseverance involved.
- **Share Stories:** Highlight examples of resilience within the organization to inspire others.

3. Promoting Work-Life Balance:

- **Set Boundaries:** Encourage reasonable working hours and discourage a culture of constant availability.
- **Lead by Example:** Leaders should model healthy boundaries and self-care practices.

4. Encouraging Feedback and Dialogue:

- **Regular Check-Ins:** Hold one-on-one meetings to discuss well-being and address concerns.
- **Anonymous Surveys:** Gather honest feedback about the work environment and culture.

Case Study 1: The Resilient Leader in Action

Meet Sarah Rodriguez, a seasoned leader with over two decades of experience in the technology industry. Sarah's journey to leadership began as a software engineer, where her technical prowess and problem-solving skills quickly garnered recognition. Through the years, she climbed the ranks, holding various roles in project management and eventually transitioning into executive leadership.

Sarah's leadership style is characterized by a unique blend of analytical thinking and emotional intelligence. She believes in leading by example, demonstrating not only technical expertise but also a deep understanding of the human element within teams. Her approach is rooted in the belief that a resilient leader must not only excel in problem-solving but also possess the capacity to navigate complex emotions and high-pressure situations.

As a leader, Sarah has faced a myriad of challenges – from managing high-stakes product launches to steering her team through periods of significant organizational change. Her ability to maintain composure, inspire confidence, and make sound decisions in the face of adversity has not only solidified her reputation as a resilient leader but has also propelled her teams to new heights of success.

Analyzing Key Situations Showcasing Emotional Resilience

Now, let's analyze key situations showcasing Sarah's emotional resilience.

Situation 1: The High-Stakes Product Launch

One of the defining moments in Sarah's leadership journey was a high-stakes product launch that held critical strategic importance for the company. The project faced unforeseen technical challenges in the final stages, putting the entire timeline at risk. In this situation, Sarah exhibited remarkable emotional resilience. Rather than succumbing to panic or pressure, she gathered her team, acknowledging the gravity of the situation while instilling confidence in their collective ability to find a solution. She provided clear guidance, fostered open communication, and worked alongside her team, ensuring that everyone felt supported and understood. Through her actions, she transformed what could have been a crisis into a rallying point for her team, ultimately leading to a successful launch.

Situation 2: Navigating Organizational Restructuring

In a period of significant organizational restructuring, Sarah faced the challenge of leading her team through uncertainty and change. The restructuring brought about shifts in roles, reporting structures, and team compositions. Recognizing the emotional impact of these changes on her team members, Sarah proactively initiated transparent and regular communication. She created forums for open dialogue, allowing team members to voice concerns and seek clarity. Through her empathetic approach, she provided reassurance and a sense of stability in a time of upheaval. Her emotional resilience shone through in her ability to maintain a positive outlook, focusing on the opportunities that the restructuring presented for growth and development.

Situation 3: Nurturing Innovation in the Face of Failure

In a highly competitive industry, setbacks and failures are inevitable. Sarah faced a situation where a key project, which held substantial promise, encountered unforeseen obstacles, leading to delays and setbacks. Rather than dwelling on the disappointment, Sarah leveraged her emotional resilience to foster a growth-oriented mindset within her team. She encouraged a candid post-mortem analysis, extracting valuable lessons from the experience. By reframing the situation as a learning opportunity, Sarah not only preserved team morale but also ignited a spirit of innovation. This resilience-driven approach ultimately led to the development of a more robust and successful iteration of the project.

Extracting Actionable Insights and Strategies

Now, let's extract actionable insights and strategies from Sarah's experiences.

1. Transparent and Proactive Communication:

Sarah's approach to transparent and proactive communication emerged as a cornerstone of her leadership style. She understood the importance of keeping her team informed, especially during times of uncertainty or change. This approach built trust and provided a sense of security for her team members. Leaders looking to enhance their emotional resilience can adopt this strategy by prioritizing open and honest communication, even when delivering challenging news. This fosters an environment of trust and mutual respect.

2. Balancing Realism with Positivity:

Sarah demonstrated the ability to balance realism with positivity. While she acknowledged the gravity of challenges, she consistently maintained a positive outlook. This balanced perspective empowered her team to face difficulties head-on while instilling confidence in their collective ability to overcome them. Leaders can cultivate this balance by acknowledging challenges while actively seeking opportunities for growth and improvement. It's about finding the silver lining without downplaying the severity of the situation.

3. Empathy and Emotional Intelligence:

Sarah's high level of emotional intelligence played a pivotal role in her leadership effectiveness. She demonstrated empathy by understanding and addressing the emotional impact of organizational changes and setbacks. This empathy created a supportive work environment and strengthened team cohesion. Leaders can develop their emotional intelligence by actively seeking to understand the perspectives and emotions of their team members. This allows for more effective leadership, particularly during challenging times.

4. Turning Setbacks into Learning Opportunities:

One of Sarah's standout qualities was her ability to view setbacks as opportunities for growth and learning. Instead of dwelling on failures, she encouraged a forward-looking, solution-oriented mindset within her team. This resilience-driven approach not only preserved team morale but also led to the development of innovative solutions. Leaders can adopt this approach by reframing setbacks as learning experiences and encouraging their teams to extract valuable insights from challenges.

5. Leading by Example:

Sarah's actions consistently aligned with her words, exemplifying the qualities she valued in her team. Whether it was maintaining composure during high-stress situations or prioritizing well-being, she led by example. This authenticity and integrity reinforced her team's trust and confidence in her leadership. Leaders can emulate this by consistently modeling the behaviors and attitudes they wish to see in their teams. It's about embodying the values and principles that define resilient leadership.

By studying Sarah's experiences, leaders can glean valuable insights and actionable strategies to enhance their own emotional resilience and leadership effectiveness. These lessons serve as a roadmap for navigating challenges, fostering team growth, and ultimately achieving success in the complex landscape of leadership.

Guided Self-Assessment: A Personal Reflection

By engaging in this guided self-assessment, individuals can gain a deeper understanding of their current level of emotional resilience, identify areas for growth, and set personalized goals to navigate future challenges with increased confidence and effectiveness. This reflective process lays the foundation for a purposeful and intentional journey towards greater emotional resilience in leadership and beyond.

Guided self-assessment to evaluate one's current level of emotional resilience, helps identify areas for growth and development and helps set personalized goals for the journey ahead:

1. Understanding Your Emotional Responses: Begin by reflecting on how you typically respond to challenging situations. Are you able to maintain composure and clarity, or do you find yourself becoming overwhelmed? Consider specific instances where you've faced adversity and take note of your emotional reactions.

2. Recognizing Patterns and Triggers: Next, delve into the patterns and triggers that influence your emotional responses. Are there recurring situations or types of challenges that tend to affect you more deeply? Identifying these patterns can provide valuable insights into areas where you may benefit from strengthening your emotional resilience.

3. Evaluating Coping Mechanisms: Take stock of the coping mechanisms you currently employ. Are they constructive and supportive of your well-being, or do they potentially exacerbate stress? Assess whether your coping strategies align with the principles of emotional resilience, and consider areas for improvement.

4. Assessing Cognitive Adaptability: Reflect on your ability to engage in cognitive processes related to understanding and managing emotions. Consider instances where you've successfully navigated complex emotional situations through thoughtful decision-making. Additionally, identify areas where you may seek to enhance your cognitive adaptability.

5. Areas of Challenge: Based on your self-assessment, pinpoint specific areas where you tend to face challenges in maintaining emotional resilience. This could range from regulating intense emotions to adapting to unforeseen circumstances. Acknowledging these areas is the first step toward targeted growth.

6. Opportunities for Improvement: Consider the coping mechanisms, mindset shifts, and communication strategies that could bolster your emotional resilience. Are there particular skills or approaches that resonate with you? Recognize the potential areas for improvement that align with your personal strengths and values.

7. Reflecting on Past Growth: Reflect on instances in your life where you've demonstrated resilience. What strategies or qualities contributed to your success in those situations? By understanding past successes, you can identify tools that may be valuable in future challenges.

8. Clear and Attainable Objectives: Establish specific, measurable, and realistic goals for enhancing your emotional resilience. These could range from incorporating daily mindfulness practices to developing a proactive problem-solving mindset. Ensure that your goals are tailored to your individual circumstances and aspirations.

9. Implementation Plan: Outline the actionable steps you'll take to work towards each goal. Consider allocating time for self-reflection, seeking resources or support, and practicing new strategies in relevant situations.

10. Monitoring Progress: Regularly track your progress towards building emotional resilience. Celebrate your achievements, no matter how small, and be compassionate with yourself in moments of perceived setback. Adjust your approach as needed to stay aligned with your overarching objectives.

Evaluating Current Level of Emotional Resilience

When reflecting on how you respond to challenging situations, it's important to consider both the immediate reactions and the lingering emotional impact. Do you tend to maintain a level-headed approach, or do you find yourself getting swept up in the intensity of the moment? Pay attention to physical sensations, thought patterns, and emotional states that arise during these times. This awareness serves as a foundational step in developing emotional resilience.

For example, imagine a recent high-pressure situation at work. Did you approach it with a sense of calm and clarity, or did you feel a surge of anxiety or frustration? Did you notice any physical changes, such as an increased heart rate or tense muscles? By dissecting these responses, you gain valuable insights into your default reactions and areas that may benefit from refinement.

Patterns in emotional responses often emerge from specific triggers. These triggers can be external, such as certain types of challenges or interactions, or internal, stemming from personal beliefs and past experiences. Take time to identify recurring situations or circumstances that tend to evoke strong emotional reactions. Are there particular themes or scenarios that consistently elicit a heightened response from you?

For instance, consider situations where you've felt particularly challenged or vulnerable. Are there common elements among these scenarios? Perhaps they involve a need for quick decision-making, navigating conflict, or dealing with uncertainty. Recognizing these patterns provides valuable foresight into areas where you can proactively apply emotional resilience strategies.

Coping mechanisms are the tools and strategies individuals use to manage and navigate emotional experiences. They play a critical role in emotional resilience, as they can either support well-being or inadvertently exacerbate stress. Take a close look at the methods you currently employ. Do they promote a sense of calm, clarity, and well-being, or do they tend to offer temporary relief at the expense of long-term emotional health?

Consider whether your coping mechanisms align with the principles of emotional resilience. Are they constructive and sustainable in the face of adversity? For instance, do you engage in activities like mindfulness, physical exercise, or journaling to regulate your emotions? Alternatively, do you find yourself resorting to avoidance or suppression? Evaluating your coping mechanisms sheds light on areas where intentional adjustments can be made.

Cognitive adaptability involves the capacity to navigate complex emotional situations through thoughtful decision-making and perspective-taking. Reflect on instances where you've effectively assessed and responded to emotionally charged scenarios. What cognitive processes did you employ? Were you able to maintain a clear and rational perspective, even in the midst of intense emotions?

Consider situations where you've had to make significant decisions under pressure. Did you approach them with a balanced consideration of both emotional and practical factors? On the other hand, were there instances where emotions seemed to override your ability to think objectively? Recognizing your strengths in cognitive adaptability provides a foundation for further development in this crucial aspect of emotional resilience.

Identifying Areas for Growth and Development

In delving into your self-assessment, you've likely identified specific areas where maintaining emotional resilience proves to be more challenging. These areas could manifest in various ways. For instance, you may notice a tendency to become overwhelmed in high-pressure situations, or perhaps regulating intense emotions is an ongoing struggle. Recognizing these specific points of challenge is a crucial first step in the process of targeted growth.

Imagine a recent scenario where you encountered a significant challenge. What were the key emotional responses and thought patterns that emerged? Did you face difficulty in maintaining a balanced perspective, or did you find it challenging to adapt to unexpected turns of events? By pinpointing these areas, you're not only acknowledging your current reality but also setting the stage for intentional development.

With a clear understanding of the areas where you face challenges, it's time to consider the opportunities for improvement. This step involves exploring a range of coping mechanisms, mindset shifts, and communication strategies that have the potential to bolster your emotional resilience. Keep in mind that there is no one-size-fits-all approach. Instead, focus on identifying techniques and approaches that resonate with your unique strengths and values.

For example, if you've identified a challenge in effectively regulating intense emotions, consider a variety of strategies that align with your preferences. This could encompass practices like mindfulness meditation, deep breathing exercises, or engaging in creative outlets. Similarly, if adapting to unforeseen circumstances proves to be a hurdle, explore techniques for cultivating adaptability and flexibility in your approach.

Reflecting on past instances of resilience provides valuable insights into the strategies and qualities that have contributed to your success. Consider moments in your life where you've faced adversity head-on and emerged stronger for it. What specific actions or mindsets played a pivotal role in your ability to navigate those challenges?

These reflections serve as a reservoir of valuable tools and approaches that you can draw upon in future challenges. For instance, if maintaining composure in high-pressure situations has been a strength for you in the past, what strategies did you employ? Were there particular mindset shifts or coping mechanisms that proved especially effective? By recognizing and internalizing these past successes, you're equipping yourself with a toolkit for continued growth and development in emotional resilience.

Setting Personalized Goals for the Journey Ahead

As you embark on the journey to enhance your emotional resilience, it's essential to establish clear and attainable objectives. These goals serve as the guiding lights that will illuminate your path forward. Each objective should be specific, measurable, and realistic, ensuring that they are well within your reach. Consider, for instance, a goal centered around incorporating daily mindfulness practices. This objective is concrete, allowing for tangible progress and measurement of success. Moreover, it is realistic and tailored to your individual circumstances.

Another objective might involve developing a proactive problem-solving mindset. This goal underscores the practical nature of your pursuit. By setting clear and attainable objectives, you're providing yourself with a roadmap for growth in emotional resilience. These objectives serve as the foundation upon which you'll build your personalized action plan.

With your objectives in place, the next crucial step is to craft a detailed implementation plan. This plan outlines the specific actions you'll take to work towards each goal. Consider allocating dedicated time for self-reflection, seeking out relevant resources or support, and actively practicing new strategies in situations where they apply.

For example, if one of your objectives is to incorporate daily mindfulness practices, your implementation plan may include setting aside a specific time each day for meditation or mindfulness exercises. You might also explore resources such as guided meditation apps or books on mindfulness to support your practice. By delineating these actionable steps, you're ensuring that your goals are not abstract aspirations, but rather concrete endeavors integrated into your daily life.

Regularly monitoring your progress is an integral aspect of the journey towards building emotional resilience. This ongoing assessment allows you to track your advancements, providing you with valuable feedback and motivation. Celebrate each achievement, regardless of its scale. Recognize the effort and dedication you invest in your growth.

Additionally, it's important to approach moments that may be perceived as setbacks with compassion and understanding. Remember that growth is a dynamic process, and it's natural to encounter challenges along the way. If you find that a particular strategy or approach isn't yielding the desired results, be open to adjusting your course. Flexibility in your approach ensures that you remain aligned with your overarching objectives as you continue on your path towards enhanced emotional resilience.

Cultivating Foundational Resilience Traits

Emotional resilience is not an inherent trait but a set of skills and characteristics that can be developed and strengthened over time. These foundational traits empower individuals to navigate challenges with composure, adaptability, and effectiveness. By cultivating these qualities, leaders and individuals alike can enhance their capacity to bounce back from adversity and thrive in the face of life's complexities.

1. Self-Awareness

Understanding Self-Awareness

At the core of emotional resilience lies self-awareness—the ability to recognize and understand one's own emotions, thoughts, and values, and how they influence behavior. Self-aware individuals are attuned to their emotional states and can identify triggers that may affect their responses to stress or adversity.

Importance in Emotional Resilience

Emotional Regulation: Self-awareness is the first step toward regulating emotions. By recognizing feelings as they arise, individuals can choose how to respond rather than reacting impulsively.

Authenticity: Understanding oneself leads to more authentic interactions with others, fostering trust and genuine relationships.

Decision-Making: Self-aware leaders make more informed decisions, as they can separate personal biases from objective analysis.

Strategies to Cultivate Self-Awareness

Mindfulness Practices: Engage in mindfulness meditation or deep-breathing exercises to increase present-moment awareness.

Reflective Journaling: Regularly write about your thoughts and feelings to identify patterns and gain insights into your emotional landscape.

Seek Feedback: Ask trusted colleagues, mentors, or friends for honest feedback about your behavior and its impact on others.

Self-Assessment Tools: Use tools like William Stanek's Resilient Growth Self-Assessment and the 8 Pillars of Leadership: Self-Assessment to deepen your understanding of yourself.

Example:

Nelson Mandela demonstrated profound self-awareness during his 27 years of imprisonment. By reflecting on his beliefs and emotions, he emerged with a strong sense of purpose and the ability to lead South Africa toward reconciliation and unity.

2. Adaptability

Understanding Adaptability

Adaptability is the capacity to adjust effectively to new conditions, unexpected challenges, or changing environments. It involves flexibility in thinking and behavior, allowing individuals to pivot strategies when circumstances shift.

Importance in Emotional Resilience

Navigating Change: Adaptable individuals handle transitions smoothly, reducing stress associated with uncertainty.

Innovation: Flexibility encourages creative problem-solving and openness to new ideas.

Resilience to Setbacks: Adaptability enables quicker recovery from disappointments or failures.

Strategies to Cultivate Adaptability

Embrace a Growth Mindset: View challenges as opportunities to learn rather than obstacles. Believe in your ability to develop new skills.

Expose Yourself to New Experiences: Stepping out of your comfort zone enhances your ability to handle unfamiliar situations.

Practice Cognitive Flexibility: Challenge your assumptions and consider multiple perspectives when addressing problems.

Set Flexible Goals: While having clear objectives is important, remain open to adjusting your plans as needed.

Example:

Indra Nooyi, as CEO of PepsiCo, navigated the company through significant shifts by adapting the business strategy toward healthier products in response to changing consumer preferences. Her adaptability was key to sustaining the company's growth.

3. Proactive Problem-Solving

Understanding Proactive Problem-Solving

A proactive problem-solving orientation involves anticipating potential challenges and taking initiative to address them before they escalate. It reflects a mindset focused on action and solution-seeking rather than passivity or avoidance.

Importance in Emotional Resilience

Empowerment: Taking proactive steps fosters a sense of control over situations, reducing feelings of helplessness.

Efficiency: Early intervention can prevent small issues from becoming major problems.

Confidence: Successfully navigating challenges enhances self-efficacy and resilience.

Strategies to Cultivate Proactive Problem-Solving

Anticipate Challenges: Regularly assess potential obstacles in your projects or goals and plan accordingly.

Set Actionable Steps: Break down problems into manageable tasks with clear next steps.

Cultivate Curiosity: Ask questions and seek knowledge to better understand complex situations.

Develop Decision-Making Skills: Practice making timely decisions, even when information is incomplete.

Example:

Elon Musk exemplifies proactive problem-solving through his ventures like SpaceX and Tesla. By anticipating future challenges such as sustainable energy and space exploration, he actively works toward innovative solutions that address global issues.

4. Inner Strength

Understanding Inner Strength

Inner strength refers to the deep-seated resilience and confidence that enable individuals to persevere through difficulties. It encompasses courage, determination, and a steadfast belief in one's abilities and values.

Importance in Emotional Resilience

Perseverance: Inner strength fuels the persistence needed to overcome obstacles and achieve long-term goals.

Composure: It helps maintain emotional stability during crises or high-pressure situations.

Self-Belief: A strong inner core bolsters confidence, reducing susceptibility to doubt or external negativity.

Strategies to Cultivate Inner Strength

Reflect on Past Successes: Recall times when you overcame challenges to reinforce your ability to handle adversity.

Set Personal Values: Clearly define your principles and let them guide your actions and decisions.

Practice Self-Compassion: Treat yourself with kindness and understanding during difficult times.

Build Resilience Through Challenges: Embrace hardships as opportunities to strengthen your character and capabilities.

Example:

Malala Yousafzai, the youngest Nobel Peace Prize laureate, showcases profound inner strength. After surviving an assassination attempt for advocating girls' education, she continued her activism with even greater determination, inspiring millions worldwide.

Integrating Foundational Traits: Strategies for Development

Developing these foundational traits requires intentional effort and consistent practice. Here are strategies to actively cultivate self-awareness, adaptability, proactive problem-solving, and inner strength:

1. Embrace Change as an Opportunity

Shift Perspective: Reframe changes as chances to grow rather than threats to stability.

Set Learning Goals: Identify what you can gain from new experiences or challenges.

Stay Informed: Keep up-to-date with industry trends to anticipate and prepare for changes.

Action Step: When faced with a change, list potential benefits and new skills you can acquire as a result.

2. Practice Mindful Awareness

Daily Mindfulness Exercises: Dedicate time each day to mindfulness meditation or breathing techniques to enhance present-moment awareness.

Emotional Check-Ins: Regularly pause to assess your emotional state and acknowledge your feelings without judgment.

Mindful Listening: Pay full attention during conversations, which enhances empathy and understanding.

Action Step: Start a mindfulness journal to record your thoughts, feelings, and observations about your experiences.

3. Seek Constructive Solutions

Adopt a Solutions-Focused Approach: Instead of dwelling on problems, immediately begin brainstorming possible solutions.

Collaborate with Others: Engage team members or peers in problem-solving to gain diverse perspectives.

Use Problem-Solving Frameworks: Apply methodologies like GROW analysis (Gains, Realities, Opportunities, Weaknesses) to structure your approach.

Action Step: When a problem arises, write down at least three possible solutions before taking action.

4. Draw on Past Resilience

Create a Resilience Timeline: Document past challenges you've overcome and the strengths you utilized.

Identify Resilience Skills: Recognize specific skills or traits that helped you succeed in previous situations.

Build a Personal Affirmation: Develop a mantra or statement that reinforces your resilience and can be recalled during tough times.

Action Step: Reflect on a significant past challenge and write about how you overcame it, focusing on the inner strengths you employed.

5. Cultivate a Growth Mindset

Embrace Lifelong Learning: Continuously seek new knowledge and skills through courses, reading, or workshops.

Challenge Fixed Beliefs: Identify and question any limiting beliefs about your abilities.

Celebrate Effort: Acknowledge the hard work and process involved in tasks, not just the outcomes.

Action Step: Set a learning goal outside your comfort zone, such as mastering a new language or technical skill.

6. Cultivate a Supportive Network

Seek Mentorship: Find mentors who exemplify the traits you wish to develop and learn from their experiences.

Build Relationships: Nurture connections with peers who are supportive and share similar goals.

Engage in Communities: Join professional groups or online forums related to your interests and fields.

Action Step: Reach out to someone you admire and request a meeting or conversation to gain insights and advice.

The Synergy of Foundational Traits

These foundational traits do not exist in isolation but are interconnected and mutually reinforcing:

- **Self-Awareness Enhances Adaptability:** Understanding your emotions and triggers allows you to adjust your responses to new situations more effectively.
- **Adaptability Fuels Proactive Problem-Solving:** Being open to change enables you to anticipate challenges and develop solutions proactively.
- **Proactive Problem-Solving Strengthens Inner Strength:** Successfully addressing challenges builds confidence and reinforces your inner resilience.
- **Inner Strength Supports Self-Awareness:** A strong sense of self provides the courage to explore and understand your inner world deeply.

Example in Practice:

Consider Dr. Wangari Maathai, the Kenyan environmentalist and Nobel Peace Prize laureate. She:

- **Exhibited Self-Awareness:** Recognized her passion for the environment and social justice.
- **Demonstrated Adaptability:** Navigated political opposition and adjusted her strategies to promote sustainable development.
- **Engaged in Proactive Problem-Solving:** Founded the Green Belt Movement to address deforestation and empower communities.

- **Drew on Inner Strength:** Persisted despite arrests and intimidation, driven by her unwavering commitment to her cause.

Her integrated use of these foundational traits led to significant environmental and social impact in Kenya and worldwide.

—

By actively cultivating self-awareness, adaptability, proactive problem-solving, and inner strength, individuals lay a robust foundation for emotional resilience. These traits empower leaders and professionals to face adversity with confidence, navigate change gracefully, and inspire others through their example.

Integrating the strategies outlined above into daily life fosters continuous growth and prepares individuals to handle life's complexities effectively. Emotional resilience is not a destination but an ongoing journey of self-development and empowerment, leading to personal fulfillment and professional excellence.

Next Steps:
- **Personal Assessment:** Take time to evaluate which foundational traits you excel in and which may need further development.
- **Set Specific Goals:** Identify concrete actions you will take to cultivate each trait.
- **Reflect Regularly:** Schedule periodic reflections to assess your progress and adjust your strategies as needed.

By committing to this process, you not only enhance your own resilience but also contribute positively to your organization and community.

Building a Resilient Mindset

A resilient mindset is the cornerstone of emotional resilience, enabling individuals to navigate challenges with grace, determination, and a sense of purpose. It represents a shift from reactive responses to proactive, forward-thinking approaches. Cultivating this mindset empowers leaders not only to weather adversity but to thrive amid it, transforming obstacles into opportunities for growth and innovation.

1. Shifting from Reactive to Proactive

Understanding the Shift

Reactive Mindset: Characterized by responding to situations only after they occur, often driven by immediate emotions or external pressures. This approach can lead to feeling overwhelmed or out of control.

Proactive Mindset: Involves anticipating challenges, identifying opportunities, and taking preemptive action. Leaders with a proactive mindset shape outcomes and influence their environment rather than merely reacting to it.

Why It Matters

Control Over Outcomes: Proactive leaders are better positioned to influence results positively.

Enhanced Preparedness: Anticipating challenges allows for contingency planning and reduces the impact of unexpected events.

Improved Decision-Making: Proactivity encourages strategic thinking and long-term planning.

Strategies to Shift Mindsets

Set Aside Time for Strategic Planning: Regularly dedicate time to assess goals, potential obstacles, and opportunities.

Develop Situational Awareness: Stay informed about industry trends, competitor actions, and global events that could impact your organization.

Cultivate Initiative: Encourage yourself and team members to propose ideas and take action without waiting for directives.

Example:

Consider Sheryl Sandberg, COO of Facebook, who has demonstrated a proactive mindset in her leadership. After experiencing personal tragedy, she proactively addressed the challenges by co-authoring the book "Option B," focusing on building resilience. Her proactive approach not only helped her navigate her own grief but also provided valuable insights to others facing adversity.

2. Embracing Challenges as Opportunities for Growth

Rather than viewing challenges as obstacles, a resilient mindset reframes them as opportunities for learning and development. This perspective encourages leaders to seek out and embrace new experiences, even if they entail uncertainty or discomfort. It fosters a sense of empowerment and a willingness to take calculated risks.

Understanding the Perspective

Fixed Mindset vs. Growth Mindset: Coined by psychologist Carol Dweck, a fixed mindset views abilities as static, while a growth mindset sees them as qualities that can be developed.

Reframing Challenges: Viewing difficulties as catalysts for learning encourages resilience and adaptability.

Benefits

Enhanced Learning: Challenges push individuals to acquire new skills and knowledge.

Increased Innovation: Difficult situations often require creative solutions, fostering innovation.

Personal Development: Overcoming obstacles builds confidence and expands one's capabilities.

Strategies to Embrace Challenges

Reflect on Past Successes: Recall previous challenges you overcame and the growth that resulted.

Set Stretch Goals: Aim for objectives that push you beyond your comfort zone.

Adopt Positive Language: Replace negative self-talk with empowering affirmations.

Example:

When Jack Ma, founder of Alibaba Group, faced repeated rejections early in his career, he embraced these setbacks as learning experiences. His perseverance and willingness to grow from challenges led to the creation of one of the world's largest e-commerce companies.

3. Cultivating a Forward-Thinking Perspective

A forward-thinking perspective involves considering the long-term implications of decisions and actions. It requires leaders to envision future scenarios, anticipate trends, and strategize accordingly. This proactive orientation enables leaders to position themselves and their teams for success in an ever-evolving landscape.

Understanding Forward-Thinking

Long-Term Vision: Envisioning future scenarios and planning accordingly.

Anticipation of Trends: Staying ahead of industry changes and societal shifts.

Strategic Alignment: Ensuring that daily actions contribute to overarching goals.

Importance

Sustainable Success: Forward-thinking leaders position their organizations for long-term viability.

Competitive Advantage: Anticipating market trends allows for timely innovation.

Resource Optimization: Aligning resources with future objectives prevents wasted effort.

Strategies to Develop Forward-Thinking

Engage in Scenario Planning: Explore various future possibilities and prepare for them.

Continuous Learning: Stay informed through reading, attending conferences, and networking.

Encourage Diverse Perspectives: Gather input from a wide range of sources to broaden understanding.

Example:

Under the leadership of Satya Nadella, Microsoft shifted its focus to cloud computing and AI, anticipating the future direction of technology. This forward-thinking approach revitalized the company and positioned it as a leader in emerging tech spaces.

Strategies to Cultivate a Resilient Mindset

Building a resilient mindset requires intentional effort and consistent practice. The following strategies offer practical approaches to develop this essential aspect of emotional resilience:

1. Practice Mindfulness and Reflection

Engage in mindfulness practices to enhance self-awareness and gain clarity on your thought processes and reactions. Regular reflection allows you to identify areas where a proactive mindset can be applied.

Purpose: Enhance self-awareness and gain clarity on thought processes and reactions.

Methods:

Mindfulness Meditation: Regular meditation improves focus and emotional regulation.

Reflective Journaling: Writing about experiences and feelings helps identify patterns and areas for growth.

Mindful Breathing Exercises: Simple techniques to reduce stress and center the mind.

Benefits

Improved Emotional Regulation: Better control over responses to stressors.

Increased Self-Awareness: Deeper understanding of one's motivations and behaviors.

Enhanced Focus: Ability to concentrate on present tasks without distraction.

Example:

Leaders like Arianna Huffington advocate for mindfulness practices to improve well-being and performance. Incorporating mindfulness into her routine helped her recover from burnout and led her to found Thrive Global, promoting well-being and productivity.

2. Set Clear Goals and Objectives

Establish clear, actionable goals that align with your vision and values. This provides a roadmap for proactive decision-making and ensures that actions are driven by purpose.

Purpose: Provide a roadmap for proactive decision-making and purposeful actions.

Methods:

WISE Goals: Well-Defined, Inspiring, Sustainable, and Empowering objectives.

Vision Statements: Articulate a clear picture of desired future outcomes.

Regular Progress Reviews: Assess and adjust goals as needed.

Benefits

Direction and Focus: Clear goals guide daily actions and decisions.

Motivation: Defined objectives provide motivation and a sense of purpose.

Accountability: Tracking progress encourages responsibility and commitment.

Example:

Elon Musk's clear objectives for SpaceX—to reduce space transportation costs and enable the colonization of Mars—drive the company's strategic decisions and innovative efforts.

3. Anticipate Challenges and Contingencies

Take a proactive approach to identifying potential challenges and developing contingency plans. This preparation minimizes the impact of unforeseen events and allows for swift, effective responses.

Purpose: Minimize the impact of unforeseen events through preparation.

Methods:

Risk Assessment: Identify potential risks and their likelihood.

Contingency Planning: Develop backup plans for critical scenarios.

Environmental Scanning: Monitor external factors that could affect goals.

Benefits:

Reduced Uncertainty: Preparation alleviates anxiety about the unknown.

Swift Response: Ready plans enable quick action when challenges arise.

Resilience: Ability to adapt plans maintains momentum toward goals.

Example:

Businesses that had contingency plans for remote work were better equipped to handle the sudden shift caused by the COVID-19 pandemic, demonstrating the value of anticipating challenges.

4. Foster a Learning Culture

Encourage a culture of continuous learning and development within your team or organization. Emphasize the value of seeking out new knowledge and experiences as a means of building resilience.

Purpose: Encourage continuous development and adaptability within the team or organization.

Methods:

Professional Development Opportunities: Provide training, workshops, and educational resources.

Knowledge Sharing: Promote collaboration and exchange of ideas.

Learning from Mistakes: Analyze failures to extract lessons and improve processes.

Benefits:

Enhanced Innovation: Continuous learning fuels creativity and new solutions.

Employee Engagement: Opportunities for growth increase job satisfaction.

Organizational Agility: A learning culture adapts more readily to change.

Example:

Google's culture encourages employees to spend a portion of their time on projects outside their core responsibilities, fostering innovation and personal growth.

5. Embody Adaptability and Flexibility

Demonstrate adaptability in your leadership style and decision-making processes. This not only sets an example for your team but also allows you to respond effectively to changing circumstances.

Purpose: Respond effectively to changing circumstances and set an example for others.

Methods:

Flexible Leadership Styles: Adjust approach based on team needs and situational demands.

Open-Mindedness: Remain receptive to new ideas and alternative perspectives.

Embrace Change: View adjustments as opportunities rather than inconveniences.

Benefits:

Improved Problem-Solving: Flexibility allows for creative solutions.

Team Cohesion: Adaptive leaders can better support their teams through transitions.

Sustained Performance: Flexibility ensures continued progress despite obstacles.

Example:

When Netflix transitioned from DVD rentals to streaming services, leadership's adaptability was crucial in redefining the company's business model and maintaining its relevance.

6. Celebrate Small Wins

Acknowledge and celebrate achievements, no matter how incremental. Recognizing progress reinforces a proactive mindset and provides motivation for continued growth.

Purpose: Reinforce a proactive mindset and maintain motivation through recognition of progress.

Methods:

Acknowledge Achievements: Publicly recognize individual and team accomplishments.

Reflect on Progress: Regularly review milestones reached toward larger goals.

Reward Effort: Celebrate not just outcomes but the dedication and hard work involved.

Benefits:

Boosted Morale: Recognition increases satisfaction and encourages continued effort.

Momentum: Celebrating progress propels teams forward.

Positive Reinforcement: Encourages behaviors aligned with organizational values and objectives.

Example:

Sales teams often use small incentives and recognition programs to celebrate meeting interim targets, keeping motivation high throughout longer sales cycles.

Integrating the Strategies

To effectively build a resilient mindset, leaders should integrate these strategies into their daily practices and organizational culture:

- **Lead by Example:** Demonstrate the resilient behaviors you wish to see in your team.
- **Encourage Participation:** Involve team members in goal-setting and problem-solving processes.
- **Provide Support:** Offer resources and assistance to help others develop resilience.
- **Monitor and Adjust:** Regularly assess the effectiveness of strategies and make necessary adjustments.

—

Cultivating a resilient mindset is a transformative process that empowers leaders and their teams to navigate the complexities of modern challenges effectively. By shifting from reactive to proactive approaches, embracing challenges as growth opportunities, and cultivating a forward-thinking perspective, individuals can enhance their emotional resilience and overall leadership effectiveness.

Implementing strategies such as practicing mindfulness, setting clear goals, anticipating challenges, fostering a learning culture, embodying adaptability, and celebrating small wins creates a solid foundation for this mindset. As leaders consciously integrate these practices, they not only strengthen their capacity to overcome adversity but also inspire and equip those around them to do the same.

A resilient mindset is not just about enduring hardships; it's about leveraging every experience to grow stronger, wiser, and more capable. In an ever-evolving landscape, this mindset is essential for enduring success and fostering a thriving, dynamic organization poised to meet the future with confidence.

Resilience as a Leadership Competency

In today's dynamic and rapidly evolving business landscape, emotional resilience has emerged as a critical leadership competency. It equips leaders with the capacity to navigate complex challenges, inspire confidence in their teams, and drive organizational success. Recognizing and developing emotional resilience as a core leadership skill is essential for effectively steering teams and organizations through the uncertainties and pressures of the modern business environment.

1. Recognizing Emotional Resilience as a Critical Leadership Skill

From Soft Skill to Strategic Necessity

Emotional resilience is no longer merely a "soft skill" or a desirable trait—it's a strategic necessity for effective leadership. As businesses face increasing volatility, uncertainty, complexity, and ambiguity (VUCA), leaders must possess the ability to:

Maintain Composure: Stay calm and collected in the face of adversity, preventing panic and fostering rational responses.

Make Informed Decisions: Analyze situations objectively, even under pressure, to ensure decisions align with organizational goals.

Inspire Teams: Motivate and reassure team members, fostering trust and confidence during challenging times.

The Evolving Business Landscape

Globalization, technological advancements, and rapid market shifts demand leaders who can adapt quickly and effectively. Emotional resilience enables leaders to:

Navigate Change: Adjust strategies proactively in response to market dynamics.

Lead Through Crisis: Provide steady guidance during organizational upheavals or external disruptions.

Drive Innovation: Encourage a culture that embraces new ideas and continuous improvement.

Research Insight

Studies have shown that organizations led by emotionally resilient leaders are more likely to:

- Achieve higher levels of employee engagement.
- Exhibit greater adaptability to market changes.
- Sustain long-term performance and profitability.

2. Impact on Decision-Making

Clarity Under Pressure

Emotional resilience directly influences a leader's decision-making process. In high-pressure situations, stress and emotions can cloud judgment. Emotionally resilient leaders are better equipped to:

Regulate Emotions: Recognize and manage their stress responses to maintain clarity.

Assess Risks Objectively: Evaluate potential risks and benefits without bias.

Implement Strategic Thinking: Focus on long-term implications rather than short-term fixes.

Avoiding Common Pitfalls

Leaders lacking emotional resilience may fall victim to:

Decision Paralysis: Inability to make timely decisions due to overwhelming stress.

Impulsive Actions: Making rash decisions driven by fear or anxiety.

Groupthink: Succumbing to peer pressure rather than critically evaluating options.

Example:

As the President of Taiwan, Tsai Ing-wen has demonstrated emotional resilience in her leadership, particularly during the COVID-19 pandemic. Her proactive approach included swift public health measures and transparent communication, balancing public health concerns with economic implications. Her ability to maintain composure and make informed decisions under pressure contributed to Taiwan's effective response to the crisis.

3. Influence on Team Dynamics

Setting the Organizational Tone

Leaders with strong emotional resilience have a transformative impact on team dynamics by:

Demonstrating Positivity: Approaching challenges with optimism, boosting team morale.

Modeling Resilience: Serving as a blueprint for how team members should handle adversity.

Fostering Open Communication: Creating an environment where team members feel safe to express ideas and concerns.

Inspiring Determination and Resolve

Emotionally resilient leaders inspire their teams to:

Embrace Challenges: View obstacles as opportunities for growth.

Collaborate Effectively: Work together to find innovative solutions.

Stay Committed: Maintain focus and dedication despite setbacks.

Building Trust and Cohesion

By managing their emotions effectively, leaders build trust within their teams, enhancing:

Team Cohesion: Strengthening relationships among team members.

Employee Engagement: Increasing commitment to organizational goals.

Collective Performance: Improving overall productivity and effectiveness.

Example:

As CEO of Microsoft, Satya Nadella transformed the company's culture by fostering empathy, collaboration, and a growth mindset. His emotional resilience helped shift Microsoft toward innovation and inclusivity, significantly impacting team dynamics and leading to substantial growth.

4. Contribution to Organizational Success

Stability During Turbulent Times

The collective resilience of leaders within an organization directly correlates with its overall success. Emotionally resilient leaders provide:

Stability: Offering guidance and assurance during periods of change or uncertainty.

Vision: Keeping the organization aligned with its long-term goals.

Adaptability: Leading the organization to adjust strategies in response to evolving circumstances.

Enhancing Organizational Culture

Emotionally resilient leaders contribute to a positive organizational culture by:

Promoting Resilience: Encouraging employees to develop their own resilience skills.

Supporting Well-being: Recognizing the importance of mental and emotional health.

Encouraging Innovation: Fostering an environment where creativity is valued.

Driving Sustainable Growth

Organizations led by emotionally resilient leaders are better equipped to:

Adapt to Change: Respond quickly to market shifts and emerging trends.

Innovate: Stay ahead of competitors through continuous improvement.

Achieve Long-Term Success: Maintain performance over time despite external challenges.

Example:

Lee Kuan Yew, the founding Prime Minister of Singapore, exemplified emotional resilience. Facing the challenge of building a nation with limited resources, he maintained a clear vision and steadfast determination. His leadership led Singapore to become one of the world's most prosperous countries, demonstrating how emotional resilience contributes to organizational success.

Developing Emotional Resilience as a Leadership Competency

Organizational Strategies

Recognizing emotional resilience as a critical leadership competency means organizations should:

Invest in Leadership Development: Provide training focused on building emotional intelligence and resilience.

Encourage Self-Care Practices: Promote work-life balance and stress management techniques.

Foster Mentorship Opportunities: Pair emerging leaders with mentors who exemplify emotional resilience.

Individual Strategies

Leaders can enhance their emotional resilience by:

Practicing Mindfulness: Engage in activities that increase self-awareness and emotional regulation.

Seeking Feedback: Regularly solicit input from peers and team members to identify areas for growth.

Reflecting on Experiences: Analyze past challenges to extract lessons and strengthen coping strategies.

―

By recognizing emotional resilience as a critical leadership competency, organizations can prioritize its development among their leaders. This proactive approach not only equips leaders to navigate challenges effectively but also fosters a culture of resilience and adaptability within the organization as a whole.

In an era defined by rapid change and uncertainty, emotional resilience is not just beneficial—it's essential. Leaders who cultivate this competency are better positioned to inspire their teams, make sound decisions under pressure, and drive sustainable organizational success. As a result, businesses led by emotionally resilient leaders are more adaptable, innovative, and capable of thriving in today's complex business landscape.

Next Steps:

Implement Training Programs: Introduce workshops and seminars focused on emotional resilience.

- **Assess Leadership Practices:** Evaluate current leadership approaches and identify areas for improvement.
- **Encourage a Resilient Culture:** Embed resilience into the organizational values and daily practices.

By taking these steps, organizations can harness the power of emotional resilience to achieve greater success and foster a positive, productive work environment.

Fostering Emotional Resilience in Your Team

In the ever-changing landscape of modern organizations, the ability to adapt and thrive in the face of adversity is not just advantageous—it's essential. As a leader, your influence extends beyond strategic decisions and operational efficiency; it encompasses the emotional well-being and resilience of your team. By actively cultivating a culture of emotional resilience, you empower team members to navigate challenges effectively, contribute to a positive work environment, and drive organizational success.

The Importance of Cultivating a Culture of Resilience

Emotional resilience within a team enhances adaptability, innovation, and overall performance. When team members are emotionally resilient, they can handle stress more effectively, recover from setbacks swiftly, and maintain a positive outlook. This collective strength not only improves individual well-being but also fosters a supportive and collaborative team dynamic. As a leader, fostering this resilience requires intentional strategies and a commitment to nurturing these qualities within your team.

1. Strategies for Cultivating a Culture of Resilience

a. Lead by Example

Your actions set the tone for your team's behavior and attitudes. Demonstrating emotional resilience in your own actions and decisions is one of the most powerful ways to inspire your team.

- **Embrace Challenges Openly:** Share your experiences with adversity, highlighting how you approached and overcame obstacles.
- **Maintain Composure Under Pressure:** Show that staying calm and focused is possible even in high-stress situations.
- **Demonstrate Optimism:** Cultivate a positive outlook, emphasizing opportunities rather than dwelling on setbacks.

Example: When facing a significant project setback, instead of expressing frustration, you could convene a team meeting to collectively brainstorm solutions. This approach not only addresses the immediate problem but also models resilience and collaborative problem-solving.

b. Promote Open Communication

Creating an environment where team members feel comfortable discussing challenges is crucial.

- **Encourage Dialogue:** Regularly invite feedback and input from team members.
- **Active Listening:** Show genuine interest in their perspectives and concerns.

- **Constructive Feedback:** Provide feedback that is specific, actionable, and focused on growth.

Actionable Steps:
- Implement regular check-ins or one-on-one meetings.
- Establish open-door policies to make yourself accessible.
- Use team meetings to discuss not just successes but also challenges and lessons learned.

c. Provide Resources and Training

Equip your team with the tools they need to build their own resilience.

- **Workshops and Seminars:** Offer training on stress management, emotional intelligence, and coping strategies.
- **Educational Materials:** Share articles, books, or online courses related to resilience and personal development.
- **Access to Professional Support:** Provide information about counseling services or employee assistance programs.

Example: Organize a workshop on mindfulness techniques to help team members manage stress and improve focus.

d. Acknowledge and Celebrate Resilience

Recognizing and celebrating instances of resilience reinforces its importance.

- **Public Recognition:** Highlight team members who have demonstrated resilience in team meetings or company communications.

- **Personal Appreciation:** Send personalized notes or messages acknowledging their efforts.
- **Celebrate Milestones:** Mark significant achievements or the overcoming of challenges with team events or rewards.

Actionable Steps:

- Create a "Resilience Spotlight" segment in team meetings.
- Implement an award system for innovative problem-solving or adaptability.

2. Encouraging and Supporting Team Members in Their Resilience Journeys

a. Provide Individualized Support

Each team member has unique strengths and areas for growth.

- **Personal Development Plans:** Collaborate with team members to set goals that focus on building resilience.
- **Tailored Coaching:** Offer guidance that addresses their specific challenges and leverages their strengths.
- **Mentorship Opportunities:** Pair less experienced team members with mentors who exemplify resilience.

Example: If a team member struggles with public speaking, provide opportunities for them to present in low-pressure settings and offer constructive feedback.

b. Encourage Self-Reflection

Self-awareness is key to developing emotional resilience.

- **Reflection Exercises:** Encourage journaling or other reflective practices to help team members understand their emotional responses.
- **Guided Discussions:** Facilitate team discussions that prompt reflection on experiences and lessons learned.
- **Provide Prompts:** Offer questions or topics to consider, such as "What strategies help you cope with stress?" or "How have you grown from past challenges?"

Actionable Steps:

- Introduce end-of-project debriefs focusing on personal and team growth.
- Share resources on reflective practices, such as mindfulness apps or journals.

c. Set Realistic Expectations

Unrealistic demands can undermine resilience.

- **Balanced Workloads:** Ensure tasks are distributed fairly and consider individual capacities.
- **Clear Objectives:** Set achievable goals with defined timelines.
- **Flexibility:** Be open to adjusting expectations in response to changing circumstances.

Example: During peak periods, acknowledge the increased workload and discuss strategies for prioritization and time management.

d. Provide Constructive Feedback

Feedback is essential for growth but must be delivered thoughtfully.

- **Positive Reinforcement:** Highlight what the team member is doing well.
- **Specific Guidance:** Offer clear examples and actionable suggestions for improvement.
- **Supportive Tone:** Frame feedback in a way that is encouraging and focuses on development.

Actionable Steps:

- Schedule regular performance reviews that focus on both achievements and areas for growth.
- Use the "sandwich" method: start with a positive comment, provide constructive feedback, and end with encouragement.

Creating a Supportive Environment

Promote Team Cohesion

A united team is more resilient.

- **Team-Building Activities:** Organize events that strengthen relationships and trust.
- **Collaborative Projects:** Encourage cross-functional teamwork to broaden perspectives.
- **Shared Goals:** Align individual objectives with team and organizational goals.

Example: Host regular team lunches or outings to build camaraderie.

Encourage Healthy Work-Life Balance

Well-being outside of work impacts resilience.

- **Flexible Scheduling:** Allow for adaptable work hours when possible.
- **Encourage Time Off:** Support the use of vacation days and mental health breaks.
- **Model Balance:** Demonstrate your own commitment to a healthy work-life balance.

Actionable Steps:
- Avoid sending emails after hours to respect personal time.
- Recognize and address signs of burnout promptly.

Foster a Learning Culture

Continuous learning contributes to resilience.

- **Professional Development:** Provide opportunities for skill-building and career advancement.
- **Learning from Mistakes:** Normalize the discussion of failures as learning experiences.
- **Innovation Encouragement:** Support creative thinking and experimentation.

Example: After a project doesn't meet expectations, lead a non-punitive review to extract lessons and improve future performance.

The Impact of Fostering Emotional Resilience

By actively fostering emotional resilience within your team, you create an environment where:

- **Adaptability Thrives:** Team members can adjust to changes and unexpected challenges more effectively.
- **Engagement Increases:** Employees feel valued and supported, leading to higher motivation and productivity.
- **Innovation Flourishes:** A resilient mindset encourages creative problem-solving and openness to new ideas.
- Well-Being Improves: A supportive culture enhances overall job satisfaction and reduces stress.

—

Building a resilient organization starts with nurturing the emotional resilience of its people. As a leader, your commitment to fostering this quality can transform your team into a cohesive, high-performing unit capable of overcoming adversity and seizing opportunities. By leading by example, promoting open communication, providing resources and individualized support, and celebrating resilience, you lay the foundation for sustained success and a positive organizational culture.

Embracing these strategies not only benefits your team members individually but also amplifies the collective strength of your organization. In a world of constant change, a resilient team is not just an asset—it's a competitive advantage.

Next Steps for Leaders:

- **Assess Your Leadership Style:** Reflect on how your actions influence your team's resilience.
- **Implement Resilience-Building Initiatives:** Start with one or two strategies and gradually expand.
- **Gather Feedback:** Regularly solicit input from your team on what support they need.
- **Commit to Continuous Improvement:** Recognize that fostering resilience is an ongoing process that evolves with your team.

By prioritizing emotional resilience, you invest in the long-term success and well-being of both your team and your organization.

Case Study 2: The Resilient Leader in Action

In the realm of aerospace engineering, where innovation and precision are paramount, Björn Johansson stands as an exemplar of resilient leadership. With a career spanning over three decades, Johansson has not only witnessed but actively shaped the evolution of the aerospace industry. His journey is one of unwavering dedication, visionary thinking, and a remarkable ability to navigate through challenges that would daunt even the most seasoned leaders.

Born in Stockholm, Sweden, Johansson's early fascination with flight paved the way for his illustrious career. He earned his Bachelor's degree in Aeronautical Engineering from the renowned Royal Institute of Technology in Stockholm, an institution revered for its contributions to the field. From the outset, it was evident that Johansson was not content with mediocrity; he pursued excellence with a fervor that set him apart.

Johansson's leadership style is characterized by a unique blend of foresight and adaptability. As the Chief Research and Development Officer for Aerospace Engineering at a leading multinational corporation, he shoulders the responsibility of driving innovation and ensuring the company's technological edge. His approach is marked by a profound understanding of the intricate balance between risk-taking and calculated decision-making—a hallmark of resilient leadership.

Under Johansson's stewardship, the aerospace division has achieved milestones that have reverberated across the industry. His teams have successfully executed projects ranging from cutting-edge aircraft designs to breakthroughs in propulsion systems. These achievements are a testament to Johansson's ability to inspire, strategize, and execute on a grand scale.

One of Johansson's most noteworthy accomplishments was steering the company through a period of unprecedented global disruptions. The aerospace industry, like many others, faced the challenges of the COVID-19 pandemic, supply chain disruptions, and geopolitical tensions. In the face of adversity, Johansson's resilience shone through. He led his teams in swiftly adapting operations, reimagining collaboration in a virtual landscape, and identifying new avenues for growth.

Beyond the boardroom, Björn Johansson is known for his approachable demeanor and genuine interest in the well-being of his team members. He believes in fostering a culture of open communication and mutual respect—a culture that empowers individuals to contribute their best. This emphasis on human connection amidst the demands of a high-stakes industry underscores Johansson's understanding of the vital role that empathy and camaraderie play in resilient leadership.

Johansson's journey is not without its share of setbacks, but it is in overcoming these challenges that his resilience truly shines. Whether navigating complex regulatory landscapes, managing ambitious timelines, or leading teams through technical hurdles, he approaches each obstacle with a calm resolve and an unwavering belief in the capabilities of his team.

Next, we will delve into specific instances that highlight the transformative impact of Björn Johansson's resilient leadership. These stories serve not only as a testament to his capabilities but also as a source of inspiration for leaders across industries. Through the lens of Johansson's experiences, we uncover valuable insights into how resilience can be harnessed to not only weather storms but to emerge stronger, more innovative, and poised for long-term success.

Analyzing Key Instances Demonstrating Resilience in Leadership

Resilience is not merely a quality; it is a dynamic force that distinguishes exceptional leaders from the rest. It is in the crucible of adversity that the mettle of a leader is truly tested. In this section, we delve into key instances that vividly illustrate how leaders harness resilience to not only weather challenges but to emerge stronger and more adept at steering their organizations towards success.

One notable instance of resilience in leadership comes from the annals of automotive history. In the early 2000s, Ford Motor Company faced a crisis of unprecedented proportions. The Firestone tire recall, which involved millions of tires prone to sudden failure, threatened to irreparably damage Ford's reputation. At the helm was Jacques Nasser, then CEO of the company. Nasser's response to this crisis was a masterclass in resilience. Instead of deflecting blame or downplaying the severity of the issue, he took immediate and decisive action.

Ford initiated one of the largest recalls in automotive history, replacing millions of tires at great expense. Nasser's unflinching resolve to confront the problem head-on, accept responsibility, and implement sweeping changes throughout the organization ultimately steered Ford through this crisis.

Another instance of remarkable resilience in leadership is exemplified by Indra Nooyi, the former CEO of PepsiCo. Nooyi faced the daunting task of leading a major transformation within the company to adapt to shifting consumer preferences and health concerns. She recognized that PepsiCo's traditional focus on sugary beverages and snacks needed to evolve to align with changing market dynamics. Nooyi orchestrated a strategic shift towards healthier product offerings, investing in areas like non-carbonated beverages and nutritious snacks. This transition was met with skepticism and resistance, both internally and externally. However, Nooyi's unwavering commitment to her vision and her ability to communicate the rationale behind the transformation instilled confidence in her team and stakeholders. Over time, PepsiCo's pivot towards healthier options proved to be a pivotal move, solidifying Nooyi's legacy as a resilient leader who successfully navigated the company through a period of significant change.

The story of Elon Musk and SpaceX provides another compelling example of resilience in leadership. In the early days of SpaceX, the company faced a string of failures in its attempts to launch rockets into orbit. These setbacks were financially and emotionally taxing, and many questioned the viability of Musk's vision for affordable space travel. Yet,

Musk's unyielding belief in the mission of reducing the cost of space exploration and his willingness to learn from each failure fueled the company's relentless pursuit of success. SpaceX eventually achieved milestones that were once deemed impossible, including the first privately-funded spacecraft to reach orbit and the development of reusable rocket technology. Musk's resilience in the face of adversity has not only revolutionized the aerospace industry but has redefined what is achievable in space exploration.

These instances serve as powerful illustrations of how resilience operates in the crucible of leadership. Whether it's navigating a corporate crisis, driving transformative change, or pushing the boundaries of technological innovation, resilient leaders exhibit a unique blend of determination, adaptability, and vision. They do not merely react to challenges; they proactively shape their organizations' responses, steering them towards growth and long-term success. These stories remind us that resilience is not a static trait but a dynamic quality that can be honed and leveraged to overcome even the most formidable obstacles. Next, we will distill the key strategies and principles that underlie the resilient leadership demonstrated by these remarkable individuals, providing a blueprint for leaders seeking to cultivate their own resilience foundations.

Extracting Insights and Strategies from the Case Study

The case study of Björn Johansson, Chief Research and Development Officer for Aerospace Engineering, offers a wealth of insights and strategies for building resilience foundations in leadership. Johansson's journey is a testament to the transformative power of resilience, showcasing how it can shape not only individual leaders but entire organizations.

One of the standout strategies employed by Johansson is a relentless focus on adaptability. In the rapidly evolving aerospace industry, where technological advancements and geopolitical shifts can have profound impacts, being adaptable is imperative. Johansson's ability to pivot in response to changing circumstances, whether it be shifts in market demand or disruptions in the supply chain, allowed him to keep his team and organization ahead of the curve.

Additionally, Johansson exhibits a keen sense of emotional intelligence, a crucial component of resilience. He understands the importance of open and honest communication, particularly during challenging times. By creating a culture where team members feel comfortable expressing their concerns and ideas, he fosters a sense of psychological safety, enabling everyone to contribute their best efforts towards overcoming obstacles.

Another key insight from Johansson's leadership style is his emphasis on collaboration and cross-functional teamwork. In the complex world of aerospace engineering, no single individual or department can single-handedly tackle all challenges. Johansson actively encourages a collaborative approach, bringing together experts from various disciplines to pool their knowledge and resources. This not only enhances problem-solving capabilities but also cultivates a sense of collective ownership and responsibility.

Johansson's approach to risk management is also noteworthy. Rather than shying away from calculated risks, he embraces them as opportunities for growth and innovation. However, he pairs this boldness with a meticulous assessment of potential outcomes and contingency planning. This strategic balance between audacity and prudence allows him to navigate uncertainties with confidence.

Furthermore, Johansson places a premium on continuous learning and development, both for himself and his team. He understands that staying at the forefront of technological advancements and industry trends is paramount for sustained success. By investing in professional development programs, workshops, and fostering a culture of curiosity, he ensures that his team remains agile and equipped to tackle new challenges as they arise.

Johansson's leadership also embodies the importance of maintaining a long-term perspective. In an industry where projects often span years or even decades, it's easy to become fixated on short-term gains. However, Johansson recognizes that enduring success requires a steadfast commitment to the organization's long-range goals, even in the face of immediate challenges.

Johansson leverages technology and data-driven decision-making to enhance operational efficiency and effectiveness. By harnessing the power of analytics, simulations, and advanced modeling techniques, he empowers his team to make informed, evidence-based decisions. This not only minimizes the potential for costly errors but also maximizes the likelihood of achieving desired outcomes.

Johansson's leadership style also underscores the significance of maintaining a healthy work-life balance. Recognizing that sustained high performance requires well-rested and mentally refreshed team members, he actively encourages practices that promote well-being. Whether it's implementing flexible work arrangements or providing access to wellness programs, he ensures that his team has the support they need to thrive both personally and professionally.

The case study of Björn Johansson offers a comprehensive blueprint for building resilience foundations in leadership. Through adaptability, emotional intelligence, collaboration, risk management, continuous learning, long-term perspective, data-driven decision-making, and prioritizing well-being, Johansson demonstrates how these strategies can collectively drive success in even the most demanding and dynamic environments. Leaders seeking to cultivate their own resilience foundations would do well to draw inspiration from Johansson's exemplary approach.

Lessons in Resilience from Björn Johansson's Leadership Style

Björn Johansson, Chief Research and Development Officer for Aerospace Engineering, exemplifies resilience in leadership through a set of invaluable lessons that can guide leaders in building their own foundations of resilience.

One of the most striking aspects of Johansson's leadership style is his unwavering ability to adapt to change. In the fast-paced world of aerospace engineering, where technological advancements and geopolitical shifts can dramatically impact operations, adaptability is not just a desirable trait—it is a survival imperative. Johansson demonstrates that leaders must be willing to pivot and recalibrate strategies in response to evolving circumstances. By doing so, he positions his organization not merely to weather change, but to thrive in it.

Johansson places significant emphasis on the value of emotional intelligence in leadership. He understands that open and honest communication is crucial, particularly in times of adversity. By creating a culture where team members feel safe to express their concerns and ideas, he fosters an environment of trust and collaboration. This approach not only enhances problem-solving capabilities but also bolsters team morale, ensuring everyone is equipped to face challenges head-on.

A central lesson from Johansson's leadership style is his commitment to collaboration and cross-functional teamwork. In the intricate realm of aerospace engineering, no single individual or department can single-handedly address all challenges. Johansson actively encourages a collaborative approach, leveraging the expertise of professionals from various disciplines to pool their knowledge and resources. This not only amplifies the organization's problem-solving capacity but also instills a sense of collective ownership and accountability.

Johansson's approach to risk management is both bold and balanced. He doesn't shy away from calculated risks, viewing them as opportunities for growth and innovation. However, he pairs this audacity with a meticulous assessment of potential outcomes and contingency planning. This strategic blend of daring and prudence allows him to navigate uncertainties with a confidence rooted in strategic foresight.

Johansson is a fervent advocate for continuous learning and development, recognizing the imperative of staying at the vanguard of technological advancements and industry trends. By investing in professional development programs, workshops, and cultivating a culture of intellectual curiosity, he ensures that his team remains agile and equipped to confront new challenges as they arise.

A critical aspect of Johansson's leadership philosophy is the significance of maintaining a long-term perspective. In an industry where projects often extend over years or even decades, it's easy to become fixated on immediate gains. However, Johansson understands that enduring success necessitates a steadfast dedication to the organization's long-range objectives, even in the face of immediate hurdles.

Furthermore, Johansson leverages technology and data-driven decision-making to heighten operational efficiency and effectiveness. By harnessing the power of analytics, simulations, and advanced modeling techniques, he empowers his team to make informed, evidence-based decisions. This not only minimizes the potential for costly errors but also maximizes the likelihood of achieving desired outcomes.

Johansson's leadership style also underscores the importance of maintaining a healthy work-life balance. Recognizing that sustained high performance requires well-rested and mentally refreshed team members, he actively promotes practices that foster well-being. Whether it's implementing flexible work arrangements or providing access to wellness programs, he ensures that his team has the support they need to thrive both personally and professionally.

In essence, the leadership style of Björn Johansson imparts a comprehensive guide for building resilience foundations in leadership. Through adaptability, emotional intelligence, collaboration, risk management, continuous learning, long-term perspective, data-driven decision-making, and prioritizing well-being, Johansson demonstrates how these strategies can collectively drive success even in the most demanding and dynamic environments. Leaders aspiring to cultivate their own resilience foundations would be wise to draw inspiration from Johansson's exemplary approach.

Practical Takeaways for Leaders Seeking Resilience in Leadership

Building resilience is not an abstract concept but a tangible skill that can be honed and integrated into one's leadership style. Drawing from the lessons exemplified by Björn Johansson, Chief Research and Development Officer for Aerospace Engineering, here are practical takeaways for leaders seeking to fortify their resilience in leadership:

- **Embrace Change as a Constant:** Recognize that change is an inevitable part of any dynamic environment. Instead of resisting it, learn to adapt and view change as an opportunity for growth and innovation.
- **Cultivate Emotional Intelligence:** Develop your capacity for self-awareness, self-regulation, empathy, and effective communication. This will enable you to connect with your team on a deeper level and navigate challenges with empathy and composure.
- **Foster a Culture of Collaboration:** Actively encourage cross-functional teamwork and the exchange of ideas. Create an environment where diverse perspectives are valued, and collective problem-solving is the norm.
- **Balance Risk-Taking with Prudent Planning:** Don't shy away from calculated risks, but ensure you thoroughly evaluate potential outcomes and have contingency plans in place. This balanced approach allows for audacity without recklessness.
- **Prioritize Continuous Learning:** Invest in your own professional development and that of your team. Stay updated on industry trends, emerging technologies, and best practices. This ongoing learning equips you with the knowledge needed to address evolving challenges.
- **Maintain a Long-Term Perspective:** While short-term gains are important, it's crucial to keep your eye on the long-range objectives of your organization. This perspective provides a guiding North Star, especially in the face of immediate hurdles.
- **Leverage Technology and Data:** Use advanced analytics, simulations, and modeling techniques to inform your decision-making process. This data-driven approach enhances operational efficiency and minimizes the potential for costly errors.

- **Promote Work-Life Balance:** Recognize that sustained high performance requires well-rested and mentally refreshed team members. Implement policies and practices that support the well-being of your team.
- **Lead by Example:** Demonstrate the behaviors and qualities you want to see in your team. Show resilience in your own actions and decisions, and your team will be more likely to follow suit.
- **Communicate Transparently:** Foster open and honest communication channels. Encourage your team to voice their concerns and ideas, and provide regular updates on the organization's direction and challenges.
- **Seek Feedback and Learn from Setbacks:** Actively solicit feedback from your team and stakeholders. When faced with setbacks, view them as learning opportunities. Analyze what went wrong and use that knowledge to make improvements.
- **Prioritize Well-Being:** Ensure that your team has access to resources and programs that support their physical, emotional, and mental well-being. A healthy team is a more resilient team.
- **Delegate Effectively:** Trust your team members to take on responsibilities and make decisions. Effective delegation not only lightens your load but also empowers your team to develop their own resilience.
- **Remain Calm under Pressure:** Practice maintaining composure in high-pressure situations. This steadiness provides assurance to your team and helps maintain focus on problem-solving.
- **Set Clear Expectations:** Establish and communicate clear goals and expectations for your team. This clarity provides a

framework for decision-making and minimizes misunderstandings.
- **Celebrate Small Wins:** Acknowledge and celebrate the achievements, no matter how small. This fosters a culture of positivity and progress, even in the face of challenges.
- **Build a Supportive Network:** Cultivate relationships with trusted advisors, mentors, or peers who can offer guidance and perspective. Having a support system can be invaluable in times of difficulty.
- **Encourage Innovation:** Create an environment where creativity and innovation are valued. Encourage your team to think outside the box and explore new approaches to problem-solving.
- **Stay Resilient in the Face of Failure:** Understand that setbacks and failures are part of the journey. Use them as opportunities for learning and growth, and don't let them deter you from your long-term goals.
- **Adapt and Evolve:** Be willing to reassess and adjust your strategies as needed. The ability to pivot in response to changing circumstances is a hallmark of resilient leadership.

By incorporating these practical takeaways into your leadership approach, you can begin to cultivate the resilience needed to thrive in dynamic and challenging environments. Remember, building resilience is an ongoing process that requires dedication and practice, but the benefits to both you and your team are immeasurable.

Leadership Case Reviews: Mastering Situations in Building Resilience

Because the real world is where some of our most valuable lessons are learned, let's now look at instances that demonstrate how leaders with a strong focus on building resilience exhibit the ability to effectively navigate through crises, adapt to change, and lead their teams and organizations to recovery and growth. Their resilience serves as a source of inspiration and stability for their teams, ultimately contributing to the long-term success and sustainability of the organization.

Leading Through a Major Merger

- **Analysis**   A CEO was tasked with leading their organization through a complex merger, which brought significant changes and uncertainty for employees. The CEO demonstrated exceptional resilience by acknowledging the concerns of the workforce, communicating transparently, and providing avenues for feedback. They also implemented a comprehensive change management strategy and offered support resources for employees dealing with the transition. This approach resulted in a smooth merger process and a united, resilient organization.
- **Lesson**   This instance highlights the transformative impact of a CEO's resilience in leading through a complex merger. By acknowledging employee concerns, transparent communication, and effective change management strategies, the CEO fostered a united, resilient organization.

This demonstrates how a leader's resilience can guide their team through major transitions with stability and cohesion.

Responding to a Crisis

- **Analysis**   A regional manager faced a sudden crisis when a key supplier experienced a major disruption, threatening production schedules and customer commitments. Through quick thinking and a resilient mindset, the manager swiftly identified alternative suppliers, rearranged production schedules, and communicated transparently with affected customers. The team rallied together under the manager's guidance, demonstrating their own resilience in the face of adversity.

- **Lesson**   The regional manager's resilience in the face of a sudden crisis showcases their ability to lead effectively under pressure. Swift action, transparent communication, and resourceful problem-solving enabled the team to navigate through adversity. This instance emphasizes how a leader's resilience can inspire their team to demonstrate their own resilience in challenging situations.

Recovering from a Natural Disaster

- **Analysis**   A plant manager confronted the aftermath of a devastating natural disaster that severely damaged the facility. Drawing on their resilience, the manager mobilized resources, collaborated with external agencies, and developed a comprehensive recovery plan. They also provided emotional support to employees affected by the disaster. Despite significant challenges, the facility was rebuilt and operations resumed, showcasing the manager's resilient leadership.

- **Lesson**   The plant manager's resilience played a critical role in the recovery from a devastating natural disaster.

Through mobilizing resources, collaborating with external partners, and providing emotional support, they led the team in rebuilding and resuming operations. This instance underscores how a leader's resilience can be instrumental in guiding their team through recovery and restoration efforts.

Navigating a Regulatory Crisis

- **Analysis**   A compliance officer faced a sudden and complex regulatory issue that threatened the company's reputation and financial stability. Through meticulous analysis, effective communication with regulatory bodies, and the implementation of enhanced compliance measures, the officer successfully guided the organization through the crisis. Their resilience in the face of adversity ensured that the company emerged stronger and more resilient to future regulatory challenges.

- **Lesson**   The compliance officer's resilience in the face of a complex regulatory crisis demonstrates their ability to lead through adversity. Meticulous analysis, effective communication, and enhanced compliance measures were key to guiding the organization through the crisis. This instance illustrates how a leader's resilience can safeguard the company's reputation and financial stability in regulatory challenges.

Managing a Team Through a Global Pandemic

- **Analysis**   A department head found themselves leading a team during the COVID-19 pandemic, which brought unprecedented challenges, including remote work, health concerns, and economic uncertainty. The leader exhibited resilience by adapting quickly to the new work environment, prioritizing employee well-being, and maintaining open lines of communication. They also implemented flexible work arrangements and provided additional resources for mental health support. The team's productivity and morale remained high, demonstrating the leader's effective resilience strategies.

- **Lesson**   The department head's resilience in leading through the COVID-19 pandemic showcases their adaptability and prioritization of employee well-being. By swiftly adapting to the new work environment, implementing flexible arrangements, and providing mental health resources, they maintained high team morale and productivity. This instance emphasizes how a leader's resilience can guide their team through unprecedented challenges with empathy and effectiveness.

Recovering from a Cybersecurity Breach

- **Analysis**   A Chief Information Security Officer (CISO) faced a significant cybersecurity breach that exposed sensitive company data. The CISO responded with resilience by leading a cross-functional team in identifying the source of the breach, implementing enhanced security measures, and communicating transparently with stakeholders. Through their determined efforts, the organization not only recovered from the breach but also strengthened its cybersecurity infrastructure.

- **Lesson**   The CISO's resilience in responding to a cybersecurity breach highlights their leadership effectiveness in crisis situations. Through identifying the breach source, implementing enhanced security measures, and transparent communication, they not only led the organization to recovery but also strengthened its security infrastructure. This instance underscores how a leader's resilience can protect the organization from significant threats.

Leading Through Economic Downturn

- **Analysis**   A CFO navigated the company through a severe economic downturn, which required tough financial decisions and cost-cutting measures. The CFO exhibited resilience by conducting thorough financial analyses, exploring innovative revenue streams, and maintaining transparency with stakeholders about the company's financial situation. Despite the challenging economic climate, the company emerged from the downturn with a leaner, more resilient financial foundation.

- **Lesson**   The CFO's resilience in navigating an economic downturn demonstrates their strategic financial leadership. Thorough analyses, innovative revenue strategies, and transparent stakeholder communication were crucial in guiding the company through the challenging economic climate. This instance illustrates how a leader's resilience can lead to a more robust financial foundation and position the organization for future success.

Tools and Techniques for Enhancing Resilience in Leadership

Building resilience in leadership is a deliberate and ongoing process that involves adopting specific tools and techniques to strengthen one's ability to navigate challenges and recover from setbacks. By integrating these strategies into daily practices, leaders can maintain composure, make sound decisions, and inspire confidence, even in the face of adversity. The following are key tools and techniques for enhancing resilience in leadership:

1. Stress Management Practices

Importance:

Effective stress management is crucial for maintaining mental clarity, emotional stability, and physical health. Chronic stress can impair decision-making, reduce productivity, and negatively impact relationships with team members.

Techniques:

Mindfulness Meditation: Regular mindfulness practice helps leaders stay present, reduce anxiety, and enhance self-awareness.

Deep Breathing Exercises: Techniques such as diaphragmatic breathing can quickly reduce stress responses and promote relaxation.

Physical Activity: Engaging in regular exercise, such as walking, yoga, or swimming, releases endorphins and reduces stress hormones.

Progressive Muscle Relaxation: Systematically tensing and relaxing muscle groups can alleviate physical tension associated with stress.

Example:

A leader who starts the day with a brief meditation session may approach challenges with greater calm and clarity, setting a positive tone for the team.

2. Cultivating a Growth Mindset

Importance:

A growth mindset, as defined by psychologist Carol Dweck, is the belief that abilities and intelligence can be developed through dedication and hard work. This perspective fosters resilience by encouraging leaders to view challenges as opportunities to learn and improve.

Strategies:

Embrace Challenges: Actively seek out new experiences that push you out of your comfort zone.

Persist in the Face of Setbacks: View failures as temporary and as stepping stones to success.

Learn from Criticism: Use feedback as a valuable source of information for growth.

Celebrate Effort: Recognize and reward hard work and perseverance, not just outcomes.

Example:

When confronted with a failed project, a leader with a growth mindset analyzes what went wrong, extracts lessons, and applies them to future endeavors, demonstrating resilience and continuous improvement.

3. Time Management and Prioritization

Importance:

Efficient time management prevents overwhelm and ensures that leaders focus on high-impact activities that align with organizational goals.

Techniques:

Prioritization Matrices: Use tools like the Eisenhower Matrix to categorize tasks based on urgency and importance.

Time Blocking: Allocate specific time slots for different activities to enhance focus and productivity.

Delegation: Assign tasks to team members when appropriate to optimize workload and develop their skills.

Avoid Multitasking: Focus on one task at a time to improve efficiency and reduce errors.

Example:

A leader who prioritizes strategic planning over less critical administrative tasks can drive the organization forward more effectively while reducing personal stress.

4. Building a Support Network

Importance:

A robust support network provides emotional support, practical advice, and alternative perspectives, which are invaluable during challenging times.

Strategies:

Mentorship Relationships: Seek guidance from experienced leaders who can offer insights and advice.

Peer Networks: Connect with colleagues or leaders in similar roles to share experiences and strategies.

Professional Coaching: Engage with executive coaches who specialize in leadership development and resilience.

Personal Relationships: Maintain strong connections with family and friends who provide emotional support.

Example:

During a company restructuring, a leader might consult a trusted mentor who has navigated similar situations, gaining valuable advice and reassurance.

5. Emotional Regulation Techniques

Importance:

Emotional regulation enables leaders to manage their reactions, maintain professionalism, and make rational decisions under pressure.

Techniques:

Self-Reflection: Regularly assess your emotional responses to identify triggers and patterns.

Journaling: Writing about thoughts and feelings can help process emotions and gain clarity.

Cognitive Reappraisal: Reframe negative thoughts to view situations from a more positive or neutral perspective.

Mindful Pausing: Take a moment before responding to emotionally charged situations to prevent impulsive reactions.

Example:

Faced with criticism, a leader practices cognitive reappraisal to understand the feedback constructively, rather than reacting defensively.

6. Adaptive Decision-Making

Importance:

In dynamic environments, leaders must make informed decisions swiftly while remaining flexible to adjust course as new information emerges.

Strategies:

Gather Diverse Perspectives: Consult team members with different expertise to inform decisions.

Data-Driven Analysis: Utilize relevant data and analytics to guide decision-making.

Scenario Planning: Consider various potential outcomes and prepare contingency plans.

Embrace Agility: Be willing to pivot strategies in response to changing circumstances.

Example:

A leader facing a sudden market shift quickly assembles a cross-functional team to reassess strategies, enabling the organization to adapt effectively.

7. Effective Communication Skills

Importance:

Clear, open, and empathetic communication builds trust, resolves conflicts, and fosters a collaborative environment, especially during challenging times.

Techniques:

Active Listening: Fully concentrate on the speaker, understand their message, and respond thoughtfully.

Transparent Messaging: Share information openly to reduce uncertainty and build credibility.

Empathy in Communication: Acknowledge others' feelings and perspectives to strengthen relationships.

Clarity and Conciseness: Convey messages in a straightforward manner to prevent misunderstandings.

Example:

During organizational changes, a leader holds town hall meetings to communicate updates transparently, addressing concerns and reinforcing trust.

8. Resilience-Building Workshops and Training

Importance:

Structured programs provide leaders with practical tools, insights, and frameworks to enhance resilience.

Options:

Leadership Development Programs: Participate in courses focusing on emotional intelligence and resilience.

Workshops on Stress Management: Learn techniques for coping with stress and preventing burnout.

Team-Building Activities: Engage in exercises that strengthen team resilience collectively.

Online Courses and Webinars: Access flexible learning opportunities to fit busy schedules.

Example:

A leader attends a resilience training workshop and implements learned strategies, resulting in improved personal well-being and team morale.

9. Conflict Resolution Skills

Importance:

Effectively managing conflicts prevents escalation, maintains team harmony, and ensures productivity.

Strategies:

Identify Underlying Issues: Understand the root causes of conflicts rather than just surface symptoms.

Facilitate Open Dialogue: Encourage parties involved to express their perspectives in a safe environment.

Seek Win-Win Solutions: Aim for outcomes that satisfy all parties' interests.

Remain Neutral: Approach conflicts objectively without taking sides.

Example:

When a disagreement arises between departments, a leader mediates the discussion, helping to find a mutually acceptable solution.

10. Crisis Response Planning

Importance:

Having a well-defined crisis management plan enables leaders and organizations to respond effectively to unexpected disruptions.

Steps:

Risk Assessment: Identify potential crises that could impact the organization.

Develop Response Protocols: Outline specific actions to take during different types of crises.

Assign Roles and Responsibilities: Ensure team members know their duties during a crisis.

Regular Drills: Practice the crisis plan to identify gaps and improve readiness.

Example:

An organization with a robust crisis plan can swiftly activate protocols during a cyber-attack, minimizing damage and restoring operations efficiently.

11. Continuous Learning and Skill Development

Importance:

Staying current with industry trends and leadership practices enhances adaptability and preparedness for future challenges.

Strategies:

Professional Development Courses: Enroll in programs to acquire new skills relevant to your role.

Reading and Research: Regularly read books, articles, and reports on leadership and industry developments.

Conferences and Seminars: Attend events to learn from experts and network with peers.

Encourage Team Learning: Promote a culture where continuous learning is valued and supported.

Example:

A leader who keeps abreast of technological advancements can guide the organization in adopting innovations that improve efficiency and competitiveness.

12. Self-Care Practices

Importance:

Prioritizing personal well-being is foundational to sustaining resilience and performance over the long term.

Practices:

Physical Health: Engage in regular exercise, maintain a balanced diet, and ensure adequate sleep.

Mental Health: Incorporate activities that promote relaxation and stress relief, such as hobbies or time in nature.

Work-Life Balance: Set boundaries to ensure time for personal interests and relationships.

Mindfulness and Meditation: Practice techniques that enhance mental clarity and emotional regulation.

Example:

By dedicating time each week to a favorite hobby, a leader recharges mentally and returns to work with renewed energy and focus.

13. Reflective Practice

Importance:

Regular reflection allows leaders to learn from experiences, refine their approaches, and foster continuous personal growth.

Methods:

End-of-Day Reflections: Spend time reviewing the day's events, decisions made, and lessons learned.

Structured Journaling: Use prompts to explore thoughts, feelings, and reactions to various situations.

Feedback Sessions: Seek insights from mentors or coaches to gain external perspectives.

Action Plans: Develop strategies based on reflections to improve future performance.

Example:

A leader reflects on a challenging meeting and identifies communication improvements to enhance future interactions.

14. Delegation and Empowerment

Importance:

Delegating tasks not only reduces leaders' workloads but also empowers team members to develop their skills and resilience.

Strategies:

Assess Team Strengths: Identify team members' capabilities and align tasks accordingly.

Provide Clear Instructions: Ensure that expectations and objectives are understood.

Trust and Support: Allow autonomy while remaining available for guidance.

Acknowledge Efforts: Recognize contributions and provide feedback.

Example:

By delegating a key project to a capable team member, a leader fosters their development and frees up time for strategic planning.

15. Scenario Planning and Contingency Preparation

Importance:

Anticipating potential challenges and preparing responses enhances organizational agility and resilience.

Steps:

Identify Potential Scenarios: Consider various possibilities, including unlikely but impactful events.

Analyze Impacts: Assess how each scenario could affect the organization.

Develop Contingency Plans: Outline actions to mitigate risks and capitalize on opportunities.

Monitor Indicators: Stay alert to signs that a particular scenario may be unfolding.

Example:

A company that anticipates supply chain disruptions can switch to alternative suppliers without significant delays.

16. Feedback-Seeking Behavior

Importance:

Actively seeking feedback promotes self-awareness, identifies blind spots, and supports continuous improvement.

Strategies:

Feedback: Gather input from superiors, peers, and subordinates.

Regular Check-Ins: Schedule meetings with team members to discuss performance and areas for growth.

Create a Safe Environment: Encourage honest feedback by showing appreciation and avoiding defensiveness.

Act on Feedback: Implement changes based on insights received.

Popular feedback models include 360-Degree Feedback, the Feedforward Approach and the Holistic Feedback System (HFS) developed by William Stanek.

Example:

A leader who learns from feedback that their communication style is perceived as abrupt can adjust to become more approachable.

17. Cognitive Flexibility

Importance:

The ability to adapt thinking and approaches enhances problem-solving and innovation in complex situations.

Techniques:

Embrace Multiple Perspectives: Consider alternative viewpoints and solutions.

Challenge Assumptions: Question existing beliefs and practices to discover new possibilities.

Lateral Thinking: Use creative methods to solve problems unconventionally.

Stay Open-Minded: Remain receptive to new information and changing circumstances.

Example:

When a traditional marketing strategy underperforms, a leader explores unconventional channels, leading to increased engagement.

18. Practicing Self-Compassion

Importance:

Treating oneself with kindness during moments of difficulty fosters emotional resilience and prevents burnout.

Practices:

Positive Self-Talk: Replace self-criticism with encouraging and supportive language.

Acknowledge Imperfection: Accept that mistakes are part of learning and growth.

Set Realistic Expectations: Avoid setting unattainable standards that lead to unnecessary pressure.

Self-Care Rituals: Engage in activities that nurture well-being.

Example:

After a setback, a leader refrains from harsh self-judgment and instead focuses on lessons learned and next steps.

19. Empathy and Active Listening

Importance:

Understanding and connecting with others' emotions strengthens relationships and enhances team cohesion.

Techniques:

Pay Full Attention: Focus entirely on the speaker without distractions.

Reflect and Clarify: Paraphrase what you've heard to ensure understanding.

Acknowledge Emotions: Recognize and validate others' feelings.

Ask Open-Ended Questions: Encourage deeper sharing and insight.

Example:

By actively listening to a team member's concerns, a leader builds trust and identifies issues affecting performance.

20. Celebrating Successes

Importance:

Recognizing achievements boosts morale, reinforces positive behaviors, and fosters a resilient organizational culture.

Strategies:

Public Acknowledgment: Share successes in meetings, newsletters, or company communications.

Personalized Recognition: Tailor appreciation to individual preferences.

Team Celebrations: Organize events or activities to commemorate milestones.

Reflect on Success Factors: Analyze what contributed to successes to replicate in the future.

Example:

After completing a major project, a leader hosts a celebration to thank the team, reinforcing a sense of accomplishment and unity.

—

By incorporating these tools and techniques into your leadership approach, you can build a strong foundation for resilience. Remember, building resilience is an ongoing journey that requires dedication and practice. As you strengthen your ability to navigate challenges, you not only enhance your effectiveness as a leader but also inspire and empower your team to develop their own resilience. This collective strength contributes to a more adaptable, innovative, and high-performing organization capable of thriving in the face of adversity.

Next Steps:
- **Self-Assessment:** Identify which areas you excel in and which require further development.
- **Set Specific Goals:** Create a plan to integrate these tools and techniques into your routine.
- **Engage Your Team:** Share these strategies with your team to promote a culture of resilience.

- **Monitor Progress:** Regularly review your growth and adjust your approach as needed.

By committing to this journey, you invest in your personal growth and the sustained success of your organization.

Thoughtful Exploration: Building Resilience Foundations

These thought-provoking questions aim to stimulate reflective contemplation and meaningful discussions regarding the concepts presented. They prompt readers to explore the practical implications of emotional resilience in leadership and its interconnectedness with various aspects of intelligence.

- How do you define emotional resilience within the context of leadership, and why is it a crucial quality for leaders to possess?

- Can you recount a personal or professional experience where you observed a leader exhibiting emotional resilience? What specific traits or behaviors stood out to you?

- In your view, is emotional resilience something that can be acquired and developed, or is it an inherent trait? What informs your perspective?

- What are the 8 Pillars of Intelligence, and how do they contribute to an overall effective leadership approach? Can you provide examples of how each pillar can be applied in a leadership context?

- Which pillar of intelligence do you consider most vital for a leader to possess, and what informs your choice?

- How does emotional resilience differ from emotional intelligence? In what ways do these attributes complement each other in the realm of leadership?

- Can you envision a scenario where a leader with high emotional intelligence might still grapple with emotional resilience? How might this challenge impact their effectiveness as a leader?

- How can discerning the distinction between emotional resilience and emotional intelligence empower leaders to refine their overall approach to leadership?

These questions can serve as discussion prompts to foster contemplative reflection and meaningful conversations regarding the content we covered. They can be tailored to suit various learning environments and objectives, making them a versatile resource for diverse audiences.

For Book Discussion Groups, Reading Discussion Groups, and classrooms dedicated to leadership development, these prompts provide invaluable resources. They provide a structured framework for engaging and enriching discussions about the content, enabling participants to share their insights and perspectives.

Additional Suggestions:

- Encourage participants to draw from personal experiences or real-world examples when responding to the prompts.

- Cultivate a safe and inclusive environment for sharing thoughts and opinions.

- Consider assigning specific questions to different individuals or groups to ensure a well-rounded discussion.

- Customize the questions to align with the specific context and learning goals of your group.

Remember, the aim of these discussion prompts is to deepen understanding, foster critical thinking, and facilitate meaningful exchanges among participants. Feel free to adapt them to best serve your unique learning or teaching environment.

Enjoy your discussions!

About the Author:
William R. Stanek

Meet the Visionary, the Storyteller, and Your Guide on the Journey to Intentional Living

Biography

William R. Stanek is no ordinary author in the world of personal growth. With a background that's woven with more experiences than can be counted, Stanek is known for his straightforward wisdom, practical insights, and a talent for helping others build lives that align with their core values. His work speaks to those who seek authenticity and a real connection to their purpose, bringing an inspiring yet realistic approach to the journey of self-discovery.

Throughout his journey, Stanek has played many roles—teacher, innovator, mentor, and artist—each experience adding to the perspective he shares in his books. He is known for being the voice people turn to when conventional advice falls short and when what's needed isn't a quick fix but a path to meaningful change. Over his career, he has helped countless individuals rethink their relationship with success, personal growth, and what it truly means to live a purposeful life.

As a leader and technologist at the intersection of business, technology, and leadership, William's work extends far beyond the written word. He has spent years inspiring action, driving meaningful change, and guiding others on how to create impact that resonates, endures, and honors each individual's unique journey. His influence spans professions and walks of life, providing a grounding perspective in a world that often encourages us to chase everything at once. In this book, William shares his experiences, insights, and deep conviction in the power of intentional living with a broader audience.

Connect with William R. Stanek

Join William in exploring new ideas, challenging conventional wisdom, and pushing the boundaries of what's possible in personal growth. Connect with him here:

LinkedIn: Follow William for updates, articles, and perspectives on intentional living and personal growth.

https://www.linkedin.com/in/williamstanek/

Facebook: Like his author page for daily insights, reflections, and updates.

http://www.facebook.com/William.Stanek.Author

Twitter: Follow for thought-provoking tweets and personal growth tips in 280 characters.

http://www.twitter.com/WilliamStanek

Website: Visit http://www.williamrstanek.com to learn more about his books, workshops, and other projects.

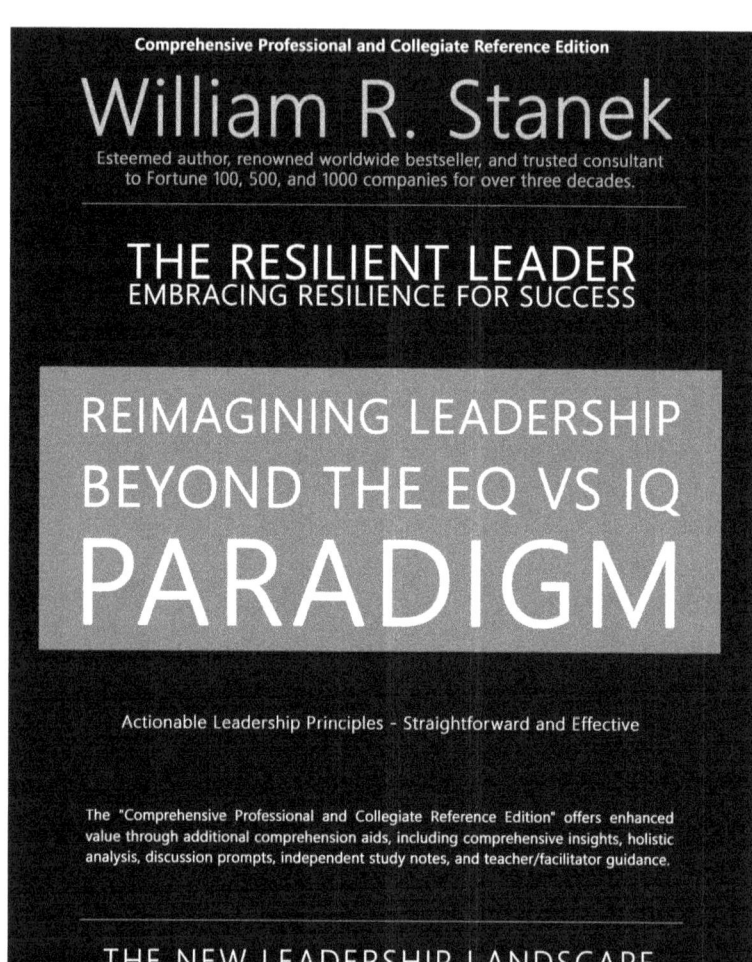

"The Resilient Leader, Embracing Resilience for Success" stands out in the crowded landscape of leadership and emotional intelligence books by offering a fresh, holistic approach to leadership that transcends traditional models. This groundbreaking work by William R. Stanek redefines the essence of effective leadership in the modern era, distinguishing itself through several key differentiators:

- **Holistic Integration of Multiple Intelligences**   While most leadership books focus on emotional intelligence (EQ) or traditional cognitive intelligence (IQ), "The Resilient Leader, Embracing Resilience for Success" introduces readers to the 8 Pillars of Leadership. This innovative framework encompasses Emotional Resilience, Creative Intelligence, Practical Intelligence, Cultural Intelligence, Intrapersonal Intelligence, Interpersonal Intelligence, Ethical Intelligence, and Analytical Intelligence. By embracing a broader spectrum of intelligences, the book equips leaders with a multifaceted toolkit, enabling them to navigate the complexities of the contemporary landscape more effectively than ever before.

- **Emphasis on Emotional Resilience**   "The Resilient Leader, Embracing Resilience for Success" delves deep into emotional resilience, offering readers actionable strategies to cultivate this essential trait. The book presents emotional resilience as the bedrock of leadership excellence, enabling leaders to withstand challenges, adapt to change, thrive in adversity, and so much more. Whereas most literature on emotional intelligence or emotional resilience treats resilience as a narrow set of traits or a subset of emotional intelligence, "The Resilient Leader, Embracing Resilience for Success" reconceptualizes it as a multifaceted intelligence in its own right. This book goes far beyond the typical definitions and presents emotional resilience as a complex, dynamic intelligence that is critical for effective leadership.

- **Rigorous Self-Assessment Tool**   Distinct from other leadership books that offer generalized advice, "The

Resilient Leader, Embracing Resilience for Success" integrates a cutting-edge self-assessment tool. This personalized assessment allows readers to evaluate their strengths and areas for growth, providing a tailored roadmap for personal and professional development. This actionable, data-driven approach ensures that readers can make concrete progress on their leadership journey.

- **Case Studies and Real-World Application** While many books on leadership and emotional intelligence rely on theoretical principles, "The Resilient Leader, Embracing Resilience for Success" grounds its insights in practical reality. Through a series of detailed case studies featuring real-world scenarios and leadership challenges, the book illustrates how the principles of resilient leadership can be applied in various contexts. From crisis management in the financial sector to navigating complex mergers and leading through global pandemics, these case studies offer readers a window into the transformative power of resilient leadership in action.

- **Future-Oriented Leadership Vision** Stanek's book critically examines the evolution of leadership theories and practices, from ancient times through the industrial revolution to the present day, offering a visionary outlook on the future of leadership. Unlike books that dwell on past or current leadership models, "The Resilient Leader, Embracing Resilience for Success" charts a course for the future, advocating for a comprehensive, adaptable leadership approach that meets the demands of an ever-changing world. This forward-thinking perspective encourages leaders to not only adapt to the new normal but to thrive within it, paving the way for a new era of leadership excellence.

In summary, "The Resilient Leader, Embracing Resilience for Success" offers a unique, comprehensive guide that goes beyond traditional leadership tenets, providing readers with the insights and tools needed to excel in today's dynamic environment. By combining a holistic view of intelligence, a focus on emotional resilience, practical tools for self-assessment, real-world applicability, and a visionary leadership approach, this book is an essential resource for anyone looking to lead effectively in the 21st century.

www.ingramcontent.com/pod-product-compliance
Lightning Source LLC
Chambersburg PA
CBHW071855160426
43209CB00005B/1061